Provide For The Common Defense

(Thoughts Concerning The Nation's Enemies)

By

Frederick B. Meekins

ISBN #: 978-1-4303-2853-7

Enemies A Real Threat To Nation

If nothing, terrorist attacks such as Oklahoma City and the World Trade Towers warn the nation that it is not without its enemies.

These maniacal undertakings strike at the very fabric of American society as they not only paralyze us on the emotional level but on the physical level as well in terms of having to evacuate buildings over concerns about suspicious packages and having to remove shoes out of fear of concealed explosives.

The memory of those children that died in these attacks who will never grow up demands that we as a nation never forget that there are those in the world who find pleasure in destroying all that we hold sacred.

It is high time liberals realize that the threat posed by these kinds of worldviews dwarf any of the dangers posed by the so-called "Religious Right".

However, establishmentarian Republicans jolly over the Cold War's end and multiculturalists intoxicated on 1970's Coca Cola ads propagating a fallacious view regarding the brotherhood of mankind both assure us that we are living in a safe brave new world.

Indeed, the world might not be safe but with the way terrorists are now permeating the heartland the average citizen is required to muster a new kind of bravery just to accomplish everyday tasks beyond the safety of one's own home.

While the United States must remain an open society, we must cast a wary eye at belligerents at home and abroad who seek our bounty without tying their fortunes to the fate of the American nation.

The axiom that the price of liberty is eternal vigilance is more than a Fourth of July platitude. It is an ever-present reminder that we must remain aware of the fact that the republic has its enemies whom we must oppose in thought as well as in deed, be they radical interpretations of Islam, renegade citizen militias, or even rogue government agencies such as the Bureau of Alcohol, Tobacco, and Firearms.

Thought War America's Weakest Front

On the sci-fi drama "Babylon 5", initiates to the elite interstellar Rangers established by the Mimbari Federation spend much of their training learning the language of that particular alien culture regardless of the recruit's planet of origin, the idea being to these warriors that combat is as much about proper thought as superior firepower. If some of the intellectual approaches applied to the war on terrorism are any indication, the United States could be headed for serious trouble down the road.

The strategic doctrine hampering America's struggle against global terrorism for the most part stems from the faulty multicultural assumptions plaguing other social institutions as well. Foremost among these fallacies ranks the notion that all societies are equal with no one culture superior to any other.

This nonsense bubbled-over onto front page news in response to comments made by Italian Prime Minister Silvio Berlusconi. Berlusconi, according to the

Washington Post, dared to enunciate, "...we should be conscious of the superiority of our civilization, which consists of a value system that has given people widespread prosperity in those countries that embrace it, and guarantees respect for human rights and religion. This respect certainly does not exist in the Islamic countries." He went on to assure that the West would ultimately triumph over radicalized Islam in much the same way as Communism was neutralized (at least for the time being anyway).

For reciting what essentially amounted to established historical fact, Berlusconi was called a "second Mussolini". In its editorial response, the *Washington Post* noted such comments were "unacceptable" and best relegated to "previous centuries". At no time was their basic factuality refuted. It must be noted that to most postmodern multiculturalists truth does not exist to begin with and has scant impact upon their style of argumentation.

Perhaps it would be best to examine exactly what was said by this European statesman. Berlusconi said our way of life was superior --- not that Musilms as individual human beings were inferior. To classify an individual as such would be contrary to the values and principles held high by the Italian Prime Minister for the world to rally around in this hour of great need. However, ways of life are a conscious moral decision and as such are subject to the standards of right and wrong or better and worse.

The last time I checked, the immigration lines were congested in only one direction. If Western nations are so terrible, as argued by a number of newspapers from the

Islamic world following the remarks of the Italian Prime Minister, why do scores of those motivated for a better life from the Middle East and Central Asia continue to flock here to take advantage of educational or occupational opportunities and assorted freedoms they could never dream of enjoying in their native lands?

Can any naive relativist honestly tell me women are no better off here than in Afghanistan under the Taliban where women were forbidden from getting an education, holding jobs or even wearing white socks, and made to feel like herded livestock every time they needed to leave their houses with the painted-over windows?

This sociological egalitarianism is not without strategic consequences. To some, it is inappropriate to root and hope for the ultimate triumph of the United States and our allies in this tumultuous conflict. It seems this error knows no geographic boundaries.

According to the *Times* of London, the National Union of Teachers there opposes the traditional lyrics to an anthem called "Land of Hope and Glory" for being "too jingoistic" in a time of international conflict for entreating the Lord with the following words: "God who made thee mighty, Make thee mightier yet." Instead, they want this sanitized as: "Music and our voices Unite us all as one... Bring our world together, Make us closer yet."

For the sake of Great Britain and the remainder of the civilized world, these misbegotten pedagogues had better pray that the Almighty makes both their kingdom and their wayward colonies mightier yet or there might not be enough of either left to sing about.

Those preferring the sappy "We are the World"

reworking of such edifying lyrics fail to realize that, should the world unite and draw together as these polemicists of pluralism propose, it will be the likes of Bin Ladin who will end up on top making the rules. For such malcontents will continue throwing their homicidal terror tantrums until they are the ones running the show.

The problem with such academic posturing is that sooner or later it weaves its way into concrete expressions of policy. A number of university administrators have spoken out against proposals to keep tabs on individuals entering the United States on student visas who either don't show up for a single day of class using this program as a pretext for infiltrating our borders or who come here to master our technology in the hopes of one day using it against us.

The University of Maryland student newspaper, the *Diamondback*, opposes restrictions curbing student visas, noting, "Diversity is never a bad thing." Such unquestioning acceptance of diversity gets you airliners flown into prominent landmarks and apocalyptic pestilences delivered with the daily mail.

Unfortunately, cognitive missteps do not confine themselves to the mental crackpots who usually administer colleges and universities and who could not land a job outside the educational establishment if their lives depended on it. Such fallacies could be winning the ears of those charged with sailing the ship of state through tricky strategic seas.

Since moral relativism teaches that no culture is better than any other, adherents by default are required to lavish the same degree of honor and praise upon them all.

This for a time led to considerable speculation in the press as to whether the U.S. would halt operations in honor of Ramadan.

Ramadan should have as much bearing on military exercises as a debate as to whether Tuesday will follow Monday, in other words none whatsoever. The matter should not even come up for consideration.

Granted, as a general rule of courtesy, it's nice to respect the rights of law-abiding citizens to practice their religion. However, these terrorists cannot be classified as "law-abiding" unless Islamic nations want to admit they don't give a hoot about American lives.

Any legitimate religion must recognize a fundamental hierarchy of values beginning with the adoration of God, respect for human beings as His highest creation, and lastly any rituals established to honor the faith in question. Honorable nations and individuals cannot violate principles higher up the chain and then hide behind the trivialities of ceremony in a vain attempt to authenticate one's piety.

It would be the epitome of hypocrisy for some lunatic to commit some ghastly atrocity in the name of Christ and then whine how law enforcement's ensuing pursuit prevented them from enjoying a merry little Christmas or relaxing Sunday afternoon.

Muslims around the world must decide if the quest to address this terrorist mess outweighs a matter God might be willing to overlook should circumstances warrant. After all, Mark 2:27 reads, "...The Sabbath was made for man, and not man for the Sabbath..." Why not the same regarding Ramadan as well?

A fundamental dogma of sound tactical theory suggests, "Know your enemy." It seems this is where the United States stands on the thinnest ice. For while President Bush is correct in noting that the United States is not at war with all Muslims, his comments that these terrorists represent only a small percentage distorting that peaceful religion for their own purposes does not quite measure up to the theological reality.

American politicians urge docile rhetoric in approaching this matter, extolling most Islamic regimes around the world as moderate nations not that much different than the United States. Yet closer examination reveals it is exceedingly difficult to differentiate between the so-called "moderates" and "extremists".

This was particularly brought to light by an article posted on the October 16, 2001 edition of WorldNetDaily.com. According to the article, in Egypt (that Middle Eastern model of democracy and individual human rights whose President Hosni Mubarak castigated the Israeli leadership as a dictatorship) Christian girls are kidnapped and raped until they convert to Islam under threat of duress. Government officials there are of little help as police intimidate and coerce Christian families under their jurisdiction into abandoning the search for their abducted loved ones.

For daring to publicize these facts in conjunction with *Whistleblower* magazine, death threats have been issued against WorldNetDaily. So much for ecumenical goodwill and brotherhood in this hour of international crisis on the part of the Muslims claiming to stand for truth and justice.

While the prudence of political realism cautions that we cannot pound into submission every regime defying our standards and values when these transgressions do not bear directly upon matters of national security, this geopolitical perspective seeking to view the world as it actually exists rather than as we would like it to be must readily admit that both Christianity and Islam are locked in an ongoing conflict whose outcome will determine the very layout of the global social order.

John Leo wrote in the September 24, 2001 issue of *U.S. News and World Report*, "...this is a global cultural war, pitting a pan-Islamic movement of fundamentalist extremists and its primary cultural enemy, America."

On September 6th, five days before the 9/11 attack, Arnold Beichman of the Hoover Institution foretold in a *Washington Times* op-ed that the current tensions between Christianity and Islam represented nothing short of the clash of civilizations thesis put forth by Samuel Huntington in the book of that same name. Beichman wrote, "Arabdom ... cannot tolerate Judeo-Christian civilization which espouses universal human rights, equality, separation of church and state, a secular rule of law, democracy, and free markets."

While President Bush is correct that not all Muslims are responsible for the acts of anti-Western/anti-Christian violence transpiring around the world, there seems to be enough evidence to suggest that the current examples of extremism manifesting themselves in terms of both rhetoric and action represent more than a minor theological aberration. It has been suggested that nearly one-fifth of all Muslims sympathize with the beliefs of the

September 11th perpetrators even if the sympathizers are themselves personally innocent of committing this historic atrocity.

Cal Thomas noted that, at an Islamic School in suburban Washington, DC, students enjoying the benefits of living in the United States were themselves cheering on the Taliban. Bin Ladin's own ex-sister-in-law admits that the Saudi regime is little more than the Taliban living amidst luxury.

One cannot help but note (and grow irritated by) the lengths taken by the government in general and the media in particular to differentiate the assorted ideological strains within Islam. Such pains are seldom taken in regards to Christianity. Usually rabid leftwing correspondents and bureaucrats can't wait to lump legitimate expressions of the Christian faith together with all manner of religious kooks and philosophical nincompoops when the perpetrators of various heinous acts happen to pop out of America's own ecclesiastical closet.

Media liberals had no problem with labeling Timothy McVeigh a Protestant when in the book *American Terrorist* it's revealed this homicidal nihilist did not believe much of anything in regards to the deity. Why the pains now among journalists for careful religious scholarship?

Columnist Charles Krauthammer has noted that, even though it was the United States that was attacked, liberal elites comport themselves as if the burden for understanding and tolerance rested solely upon America's shoulders. This is a conflict for our very survival. If the United States goes too far out of its way to spare the feelings of its enemies and their admiring enthusiasts, there might end up being very little of the United States left for this scum to kick around as we ourselves would bring about our own demise.

Linguistic Terrorism: Words Become Frontline Weapons in War For America's Future

Contemporary Evangelicals often lament the decline of Christianity's influence over American culture. Sadly, often this influence is surrendered without much of a fight.

After nearly 100 years, Wheaton College, a Christian institution of higher education near Chicago, will be changing the name of its basketball team from that of "the Crusaders" to that of "Thunder", according to the religious news website the *Maranatha Christian Journal*. The reason: capitulation to the forces of political correctness.

The name is being changed because "Crusaders" brings to mind images of the series of wars during the Middle Ages when Christians tried to retake the Holy Land militarily with less than holy methods or results. You see, Muslims find this period of world history offensive. And with the same spineless tolerance and multiculturalism characterizing the remainder of American society, a number of Evangelicals are ready to cave before the opposition, no doubt causing Charles Martel and those who saved the West from Islamic takeover at the Battle of Poitiers to role over in their graves.

Recently a group of Christian leaders from various denominations agreed to no longer use the term "crusade" in reference to evangelism efforts in a move to placate the criticism of Islamic activists.

It seems Christians just can't win. For while wishy-washy Christians fall over left and right salivating over the insights provided by the enemies of the West be they from abroad or from within our own borders, the forces of Islam seem to have no problem making their strength felt around the world through what has come to be known as "jihad" or holy war. It is sheer hypocrisy for Muslims to criticize Christians for using the word "crusade" when they themselves resort to propagating their faith through violence. For when was the last time you remember Billy Graham or George Beverly Shea planting a car bomb?

Presbyterian Minister D. James Kennedy has astutely pointed out that, in the rush to heap condemnation upon Western civilization and its accompanying history, it has been forgotten that the first crusade was actually launched by the Muslims when they embarked upon the military campaign to spread their faith beyond the Arabian Peninsula.

However, this strategy has not confined itself to history books or Discovery Channel documentaries. For while Christians stand around wringing their hands as to whom they might have offended, Muslims have certainly been busy as of late enthusiastically spreading their faith with little regard for the consequences.

One wonders if those so quick to condemn the ancient sins of Christianity will raise the ire of their condemnation against recent Islamic atrocities transpiring in the Middle East such as the lynching of Israeli soldiers, the terrorist bombing of the U.S. naval vessel in Yemen, and the 9/11 tragedies.

I Corinthians 9:22 tells us to be all things to all men so that some might be saved. But while some Christians stand around taking this Biblical injunction to ridiculous levels in an effort not be offensive to anyone, there are forces at work in the world who would like nothing better than to destroy our precious faith and to undermine our nation built upon this foundation. And if we cave so readily before them now, what sacred truths will we end up denying when they lay siege to our very doorsteps?

Pastors Display Woeful Degree of Strategic Ignorance Regarding Terrorism Crisis

Proverbs 29:18 reads, "Where there is no vision, the people perish." If a story published in the September 16, 2001 edition of the *Washington Post* regarding the kinds of sermons preached in DC Metropolitan Area churches following the terrorist attack upon the United States is any indication, it would seem that the undershepherds of these flocks may be leading the sheep considerably astray regarding the proper Christian response to these historic events causing catastrophic loss of life at both the World Trade Center and the Pentagon.

These homiletical criticisms of the nation take two basic forms. Both pretty much place the fault for this calamity and responsibility for the probable response squarely on the shoulders of the American people.

The first theological condemnation contends the

attack is judgment from God for the sin and social decay rampant throughout American society. Such argumentation is open to interpretation and requires more careful analysis.

Romans 8:28 says, "And we know that all things work together for good to them that love God, to them who are called according to his purpose."

Instead of blaming those that died, the United States as a whole, or by assigning God the negative PR which this line of reasoning ultimately does, the theologically responsible conclusion to draw would proffer that this tragedy ought to serve as a wakeup call to certain trends festering at the heart of American culture. Already the rush towards hyphenated Americanism is being reevaluated by minorities with any degree of wits about them. Already the debate has been settled as to whether or not America can withstand paralyzing reductions in its defense and intelligence resources. No longer can the United States afford to admit every teary-eyed foreigner who comes knocking on the door of our borders or (in many cases) caught breaking-in through the unwatched windows of state.

To proclaim the tragedy an act of judgment is to assume a degree of divine understanding no mortal can fully possess. The last time I checked, there are more devout Christians living within the United States than the bombed-out hell-holes of the Middle East from which this human slime oozed forth.

With the number of dead and missing in this attack being so high, it is statistically safe to say a number of committed Christians would be found among the ranks of the departed. Do they deserve to die because of some pornographer in Hollywood?

While this incident serves as a reminder of our need to rely upon God and recognize the fleeting nature of this earthly existence, one perceptive caller to C-SPAN remarked we have not forgotten God so much as these lunatic bombers have. What we have in this incident is an example of humans (in this case the terrorists) abusing their own free wills rather than an act of divine wrath.

The above matter is primarily an issue of interpretation as individuals struggle to discern the meaning of these perplexing events, and those making them such as Jerry Falwell will no doubt come on board to support an appropriate measured response. The greater concern lies with those formulating policies through more-skewered theological constructs that would inhibit the United States from taking the action needed to protect both the people and the territory of the nation.

For example, the Pastor of Hughes Memorial Methodist Church is quoted by the September 16, 2001 edition of the *Washington Post* as dichotomizing the decision faced by the United States as between peace or revenge.

The Pastor of Western Presbyterian Church in the DC neighborhood of Foggy Bottom spoke along these same lines by characterizing the path set before the nation as one of either revenge or justice. This Presbyterian went even further in his comments by classifying this atrocity as a crime rather than as an act of war. As such, a military response would be an inappropriate act of vengeance.

Obviously, neither of these clergymen lost a close

loved one in the attack.

Can anyone tell me where the justice would be in allowing Bin Ladin to live out the rest of his days in a cushy jail cell watching cable TV serving out a life sentence? These whiney peaceniks usually oppose the death penalty as well. Those preferring this course of action are so disgustingly to the left they'd probably bestow First Amendment rights upon Bin Ladin to grant media interviews and issue fatwahs from behind bars.

Those failing to see the attacks upon the World Trade Center and the Pentagon as an act of war would be forced to oppose America's response to Pearl Harbor as well. The results of such a policy would have been the enslavement of Asia by Japan, the eradication of European Jewry, and the triumph of totalitarianism around the globe if America had yielded to such dimwitted defense policies.

Romans 13:4 says, "For he [referring to civil rulers] is the minister of God to thee for good. But if thou do that which is evil, be afraid; for he beareth not the sword in vain: for he is the minister of God, a revenger to execute wrath upon him that doeth evil."

This is not to say that everything the government does is right or that those operating in its name have not infringed upon the rights of innocent citizens from time to time. But this particular incident of evil is so egregious in nature that one almost has to question the sanity of anyone standing in the way of action in terms of justice being inflicted upon the guilty.

The international arena has been called a system of "ordered anarchy". Fortunately, for now we do not have a planetary government since those running it would end up being as bad as Osama Bin Ladin or probably worse in a far more subtle way. Thus much like towns during the frontier days of the American West, occasionally just nations of goodwill must take action against the brigands on the block by running the rascals out of town or by stringing them up at sundown.

A carefully thought out response targeted at guilty parties is not revenge. Revenge is characterized by lashing out in rage blinded to all logic or reason as epitomized by those who have engaged in acts of violence directed at innocent individuals of Middle Eastern or West Asian descent. Such actions are clearly wrong, just as wrong as failing to take the military and intelligence steps needed to decrease the likelihood of these events or even worse incidents from transpiring again in the future.

Removed from much of the struggle of normal life, many pastors (especially those in denominations discounting the ravages of sin upon human nature) mistakenly assume everyone else comports themselves with the same degree of dignity, honor, and sophistication as required by their own ecclesiastical callings.

One pastor and professor remarked on the PBS program "Religion and Ethics News Weekly" that these terrorists are sinners just like the rest of us. Maybe so in the sense of Romans 3:23 which says, "For all have sinned, and come short of the glory of God." But frankly though, my own transgressions have not directly contributed to the deaths of thousands of people. One cannot insinuate that, because no one is perfect, the United States is obligated to take it easy on these mass murderers.

These fanatics do not comport themselves by the

common standards of decency that even the most licentious and decadent among us normally take for granted. Having given their lives to the ghastly goal of total revolution, one cannot reason with them as to the superiority of the Christian faith or even as to the error of their own ways. One can only annihilate them if there is any hope in preserving one's life or civilization.

It also seems a number of the pastors hostile to a pending American response fail in comprehending the role played by human activity in the plan of divine providence. The Pastor of the Second Baptist Church in Northeast, Washington told the *Post*, "...returning bad for bad is not what God has called us to do. We have got to leave some things to him."

Employing such logic, that we are to leave such things to God, it would be an act of blasphemy to seek medical attention when we are sick or even to go to work in the morning for that matter since Scripture tells us to rely on God to provide our needs. But as in the case of medical science and occupational employment, God has allowed for the establishment of certain social institutions (referred to as orders of creation by St. Augustine) through which various human needs are met. The role of government is to protect its citizens from evil doers, of which these terrorists qualify on a grand Nietzchean level.

Yet a number of these naive clergy find this essential government function appalling. The Pastor of Western Presbyterian Church in DC's Foggy Bottom neighborhood said, "It's not healthy to focus on self-defense, as individuals or as a nation. If we allow self-defense to become our number one priority, it will radically change us in a way none of us are going to like." But for what other reason does the government even exist in the first place --- to dispense Food Stamps or distribute condemns?

Over the past several decades, every conceivable special interest has postured to dominate the priorities of government, and now we face the prospect of a cataclysmic conflict that very few (both soldier and civilian alike) will end up surviving if we aren't careful. Even though civil liberties will have to be guarded in the coming days as even now desponds for despotism are slithering forth from beneath their dank borrows clamoring for the diminution of our innate liberties, it's about time officials got back to concentrating on one of government's few legitimate functions instead of contriving new ways by which to debase both culture and conscience at taxpayers expense as evidenced by past spending on the arts.

Self-defense and preservation rank among man's most basic instincts. They are nothing to be ashamed of. I bet even these pastors lock their doors at night and hold the hands of their children as they cross the street. And if they claim they don't, they are either lying or are so out of touch with reality that they ought to be defrocked for the spiritual safety of their respective parishioners.

For decades it seems, congregations have been subjected to a constant litany of missionary sob stories depicting starving children living amidst abject squalor, producing in the minds of believers a quasi-Evangelical version of Rousseau's noble savage myth where those living in these forsaken lands somehow possess more pristine character for not having been tainted by the American way of life. Christian leaders had better realize before it's too late that there are forces of evil rampaging throughout the world who will never accept our standards of decency and will do everything in their power to see that these Christian beliefs (or at least those who hold them) are eradicated from the face of the earth.

Like Father, Like Son:
Will The President Embrace His Heritage As A Wimp?

It is assumed that a president in his second term has less to lose since he is not eligible for reelection and as such possesses a greater opportunity to assert himself in terms of policy than many consider prudent for a Commander-And-Chief in the first term. In a time of war, one would assume this would mean the President would come down harder upon the enemies of the nation vowing to wipe the United States from the face of the earth.

Regardless of one's opinion of President Bush, one has to admit at certain moments in the war on terror he has spoken with refreshing bluntness uncharacteristic of a politician holding public office. However, as the President prepared to commence upon his second term he backpedaled and seemed to say some things that could be construed as embracing the Kerryite doctrine of waging a "more sensitive war".

According to President Bush in his pre-inaugural Barbara Walters interview, he regretted having said in reference to the Iraqi insurgents "to bring it on" and that he wanted Osama Bin Ladin "Dead or alive". While his feelings regarding the Iraqi insurgents are understandable in light of the tragic deaths of American servicemen serving as a testament that these savages were not as easy to neutralize as originally assessed, why in the world should anyone feel bad about wanting Osama Bin Ladin brought in dead or alive?

Perhaps we need to be reminded what this homicidal fanatic is accused of doing. Encase everyone has forgotten, Bin Ladin is responsible for killing over 3000 Americans.

Why in the name of Hades should we care if Bin Ladin and his groupies get their feelings hurt? From the impression given by the President, he might be more afraid of his old lady than international terrorists.

Thus the Commander-And-Chief feared as a cowboy in the Bolshevist press is actually henpecked and beholden to the Mrs. in a manner different only in degree and not necessarily in kind to that of the Oval Office's previous occupant. For as with the previous administration, this one also is tempted to pursue a foreign policy characterized by the female characteristics of timidity and weak-mindedness.

After receiving a verbal smack down from Laura, the spanked President said with his head down, "So I have to be cautious about...conveying thoughts in a way maybe that doesn't send wrong impressions about our country." And what "improved" image does this apology convey: that in America the President's wife is the spouse wearing the pants in the First Family?

That will certainly go a long way in striking fear in the hearts of our enemies. The only thing it will do is serve as evidence that, like the sisssified nations of Europe, the United States is decayed and ripe for conquest.

Apparently, in apologizing the President would rather America be perceived on par with France or Spain rather than as a cowboy. But whom would you rather call on in a crisis: John Wayne or Peppi La Phew?

When some scumbag breaks into your home, are you going to prattle on about the brotherhood of man and the equitable distribution of resources or are you going to do whatever it takes to get the brigand (dead or alive) off your property and away from your loved ones? The decision usually isn't difficult for real men; however, it is in all likelihood, more ponderous for European ones or those seeking their approval.

Equally naive is the President's belief that tsunami relief will improve the image of the U.S. abroad, especially among Islamic nations. For while President Bush is to be commended for realizing the threat posed by world terrorism, he fails to grasp Islam's inherent hatred of Judeo-Christian values and civilization as well as hostility to U.S. strategic interests.

In an expression of heartwarming gratitude, the Indonesian government intimated they wanted relief forces out of the country and went so far as to forbid the Marines from carrying firearms in their backwards nation swarming with terrorists and assorted malcontents. But no guns, no Marines.

The Indonesians are the ones needing the aide. It makes no difference to America what happens to such an insignificant country if that's going to be that nation's attitude.

Indonesia needs America a lot more than America needs Indonesia. They ought to be grateful for every penny we send them and should welcome with open arms military assistance as first rate and magnanimous as ours.

As a result of a desire for approval, the perceived indecisiveness of the elder Bush led him to be derided as a wimp. We can only hope the current President Bush's desire for acceptance does not compromise the need to standup for American liberties in this precarious age.

Protecting Us From Our Own Stupidity: Christians Need To Wake Up To The Real Nature Of The World Around Them

Matthew 10:16 instructs Christians to be as wise as serpents and as harmless as doves. However, it would seem some Christians would like to overemphasize the harmless side of this formula at the expense of wisdom in their approach to public policy and current events.

A guest commentary appearing in the October 23, 2000 edition of *Christianity Today* displays the type of ignorance rampant in the Evangelical community regarding international affairs, particularly in the area of nuclear deterrence. According to the article, it would be un-Christian for the United States to develop an anti-ballistic missile defense system. What ought to be considered un-Christian is such an outright refusal to acknowledge the state of the world in which we live and the proper response to it.

To say that the United States does not need such a defense is an incorrect assessment of the current strategic situation.

In support of their argument, the authors offer as evidence that North Korea is making overtures at giving up its missile program in exchange for aide in developing their space program.

And why exactly do you think they want a space program? No doubt to deploy particle beam and other satellite-based weapons the United States will end up lacking in if we follow the recommendations of these naive utopians.

It must be remembered that, even if North Korea is receiving the brunt of the justification, they in fact represent just one threat in an increasingly unstable world. Others may represent an even greater challenge but are not being mentioned for fear of upsetting the geopolitical applecart, particularly in regards to trade.

It must be remembered that these Communist and dictatorial regimes do not adhere to the same standards embodied by America's noblest ideals. Just because nations such as North Korea and Red China tell us today they now possess a greater interest in economic trade than in military conquest does not mean that will always be the case. Even then, a smile across the negotiating table could merely be cover to conceal far more maniacal intentions.

Even more disturbing than the faulty political analysis is the misapplication of Christian principles to this pivotal issue facing both the United States and the remainder of the free world.

According to Christians advocating radical

disarmament as espoused by the authors of the *Christianity Today* article, believers should respond to this kind of evil in the world by modeling the example set by Christ. The commentary reads, "A more Christlike response to the debate regarding nuclear weapons and possible warfare is to speak the truth in the face of the insanity of nuclear proliferation, regardless of what the cost might be to us."

Implementing such an idea as policy would result in disaster. Whether or not someone wants to be a martyr for the faith is their business in that Christ has His own plan for each of us. However, it is clearly out of line to impose such a position on an entire society, let alone another person. It is highly doubtful tossing Gospel tracts at the assailants would have prevented the terrorist bombing of the *U.S.S. Cole* in Yemen.

To argue that possessing a nuclear deterrent or anti-missile defense is to trust in the might of man rather than the power of God is to fall into the same intellectual trap as the Christian Scientists or hyercharismatics who consider it blasphemy to take an aspirin to cure a headache. Often God works through man to render the kind of divine protection He plans to bestow upon us. After all, one of the few legitimate functions of government is to provide for the common defense.

Christians advocating a sound nuclear policy in America's defensive arsenal are not like the radiation-scarred mutants living deep beneath the Forbidden Zone in the "Planet of the Apes" who sang hymns to and held worship services on behalf of their nuclear weapons. Rather we realize we live in a sin dominated world where not everyone adheres to the standards taught in Scripture or has the best interests of the United States at heart. And it is our obligation to protect ourselves, our families, and those too stupid to realize just what kind of world we live in accordingly.

Galactica Finale A Portent Of Things To Come In Light Of Port Developments

In the second season finale of Battlestar Galactica, the Cylons sent an emissary in the form of a religious minister genetically engineered to look human (that in and of itself an apt metaphor for many of today's churches) to the Galactica crew claiming the annihilation of the colonies of man had been a mistake and that from that point forward this cybernetic society of robots, cyborgs, and clones would no longer harass, to use Lorne Greene's words from the original series, "the ragtag, fugitive fleet".

In light of this development, the newly elected president, Gaius Baltar (himself a Cylon puppet seduced by the enemy's lusty fembot) decided to settle upon a habitable planet. An entire year elapses and it seems the Cylons have proven good on their word; however, one day from out of no where the Cylon fleet appears out of hyperspace.

Since the colonials have largely demilitarized, the Battlestars Galactica and Pegasus are forced to jump away through hyperspace with the remainder of the fleet in order to avoid detection. The episode ends with Baltar surrendering to the Cylon delegation and the metal soldiers with the pulsating red eyes marching through the struggling human settlement.

Those breathing a sigh of relief over the United Arab Emirates seeming to relinquish their claims to a number of America's most sensitive ports would do well to watch this hauntingly prescient scene.

Due to the backlash by patriotic Americans over news of a number of ports being surrendered to potentially hostile foreign powers, Dubai Ports World has promised to instead transfer control of operations to what has been labeled a "U.S. entity". Anyone saying the matter is over and the danger now passed is, to use Galactica terminology, full of felgarcarb.

For starters, what "U.S. entity" is control being handed over to? Is this a company we can trust controlled by Americans whose families will themselves be blown away should a weapon of mass destruction make it into our ports or will it be some kind of sham front American in name only but manned by foreign personnel or controlled from abroad?

And even if this port fiasco ends up settled in our favor, it's not the only threat of subversion and infiltration we face from this part of the world. According to Pastor Chuck Baldwin, Dubai has also acquired a British firm that produces parts for U.S. military aircraft and tanks.

Islamophiles will counter, but we are at peace with the United Arab Emirates. So what? Even if we are, what is to prevent them from having these parts sabotaged to prevent them from being used against their ethnic kinsman or fellow coreligionists?

Others will snap, in this global economy, we already

have foreign corporations managing vital U.S. assets. And it is a cause for tremendous lamentation.

We've already lost control over the Panama Canal and since it's controlled by a firm known for being a front for the People's Liberation Army of China, it's likely we won't be able to use it in the pending war with China likely to take place later this century.

Maybe now Americans will wake up and realize we have been lulled asleep by our news media with stories about O.J Simpson, Britney Spears not putting her baby in a carseat, and Dick Cheney accidentally shooting a friend in the face.

As the Cylon troops marched down the streets and cybernetic fighters flew overhead, Chief Tyrol turned to Starbuck and asked, "What do we do now, captain?" She responds, "Fight like we always do. Fight until we can fight no more." America's enemies will never stop plotting to bring about our ultimate downfall and that is why the price of liberty will forever be eternal vigilance.

The Haiti Mistake:
Clinton's Mission Based On Flawed Logic
(September 1994)

As with other political endeavors undertaken by the United States, the mission to Haiti has sparked renewed interest in foreign affairs at home and the role of American diplomatic involvement abroad. The primary issue surrounding the Haiti dilemma is whether the United States has any national interest in reference to this small Caribbean island.

Contrary to foreign policy idealists, the United States should only commit troops when the national interest is at stake. Both the missions to Kuwait and Panama met this criteria.

In Panama, it was necessary to unseat Manuel Noriega because of his drug trafficking and because he was a liability to the CIA. The Gulf War was in the interest of the United States because the free flow of oil was at stake along with the fragile stability of the Middle East.

Some were quick to point out the failure of the United States to remove Saddam Hussein from power. This mistake will forever serve as a reminder of the horrors that transpire when the United States bows to the dictates of the United Nations like some weak Third World nation. Hopefully, this will teach American leaders to thumb their noses at the UN and the New World Order when it is in our country's interests.

Furthermore, the United States shouldn't embark on a military mission into Haiti because of Aristide's lack of personal character and leadership ability.

Aristide is a Marxist, and as a Communist, he should not benefit from the blood of American soldiers. As a Marxist, Aristide supports the murder of political opponents and was himself a typical Third World dictator who would become one again if ever returned to power.

Aristide has also called all White men devils. Since those are his true sentiments, let him find another bunch of suckers to carry out his dirty work. Maybe he can call upon the now defunct Soviet Union or Red China since these are his ideological kinsman.

And speaking of our Cold War adversaries, those advocating strong-arm diplomacy when dealing with such rogue nations are not relics leftover from another era. Such insightful individuals realize that "please" and "thank you" seldom work in international relations.

It is much easier to dictate peace to an enemy flat on his back than at the bargaining table when he is acting like a whelp. In such instances, one must really use might to make right or at least to create the superior bargaining position.

The only reason the United States is on this mission is to increase President Clinton's approval ratings and to placate the Congressional Black Caucus, a group of Black liberals smitten by Aristide's oily tongue, for supporting the Crime Bill. Clinton hopes that the occupation will boost his approval ratings and inject his failed administration with renewed vigor to get him through the midterm elections and pending presidential campaign season.

But perhaps the most compelling reason not to go into Haiti is why should brave American forces lose their lives at the behest of an American president who fled his country to protest in a foreign land, who openly stated his disdain for the military, and who took solace in the bosom of the Soviet enemy when it was his time to serve?

The Relic Returns:
Jimmy Carter's Role As Self-Appointed State Department Foolish

With all of the media coverage afoot regarding the mission to Haiti, it seems a relic best left to history has been drug back into public view. That relic, of course, being none other than Jimmy Carter.

Despite the fact that everything is going relatively well with the transfer to "democracy" (to use the term loosely) in Haiti, it needs to be pointed out that unappointed, one-man State Departments are dangerous precedents to set in the field of foreign policy.

It seems the accolades in the press for a job well done in Haiti have all but squashed the memory of the near fiasco that occurred in North Korea. For those who don't remember, Jimmy Carter made concessions to Kim Il Sung that the United States had no intentions of backing up. In effect, he undermined the attempt to avoid a possible nuclear war on the Korean Peninsula.

Fortunately, Kim Il Sung died shortly after Carter's visit. Maybe the Carter visit was more effective than it appeared on the surface.

Comedy aside, such diplomatic guffaws cannot be tolerated on a regular basis. Diplomatic personnel and ambassadors working under the tight reins of the President and the government should be the one crafting official U.S. foreign policy.

Fortunately, the President eventually sent Sam Nunn and Colin Powell to keep this loose canon with massive teeth and the smell of peanuts on his breath in check. It was no doubt Colin Powell's careful enunciation of the forces that would overwhelm Haiti that did more to enlist General Cedras' cooperation than did Carter's southern charm.

Contrary to the warm and fuzzy notions of the New World Order crowd, the post-Cold War world is not a place where the enemies of the United States celebrate the common brotherhood of all mankind. If anything, the world has become a more ominous place since the "collapse" of the Soviet Union due to the proliferation of nuclear weapons, terrorism on our own soil, and industrial espionage conducted against the United States by so-called allies such as France.

While diplomacy is preferable to war, a sharp set of teeth must accompany a wide smile if we are to win the day. Men like Raul Cedras and Saddam Hussein only understand brute force. To think otherwise is a betrayal of the hard lesson learned by Neville Chamberlain when he mistakenly uttered "Peace in our time."

Rogue diplomats like Jimmy Carter only undermine the efforts of sovereign nations resigned to this reality and who are resolved to uphold this principle. His efforts to lobby the United Nations Security Council against the Gulf War could have derailed the coalition that allowed for the successful expulsion of Iraq from Kuwait.

Other than the Camp David Accords, Mr. Carter's foreign policy achievements were dubious at best. What else was there; that ridiculous convention on the rights of women that was drafted by social engineers and resubmitted to the Senate during the Clinton

Administration?

If ratified, international treaties such as that would pose a serious threat to the family and the minds of children, not to mention what they would do to national sovereignty. The relationship between the sexes within the United States is the business of the United States and not some busybody at UNESCO.

Jimmy Carter should stay out of U.S. foreign policy and stick to building shacks for the poor and other vagrants. Apparently, it's the only thing he is not all thumbs at, and that's only true if he doesn't pound one of them with a hammer while hammering a nail.

World Bank Protests:
Democracy In Action Or Hooliganism?

In the aftermath of protests against the World Bank, pundits and policymakers must sift through these events in order to decrease their likelihood of occurring again. Incorrectly assessing the nature of such phenomena will do little in preventing similar social upheaval sometime in the future.

In a commentary appearing in the *Prince George's Journal*, Thomas Mooney characterized the World Bank protestors as an example of the positive grassroots democracy healthy for the American political system. Such an assessment is sadly mistaken and does not characterize what actually took place.

While the Constitution does ensure the right to assemble and to petition for the redress of grievances, somehow I don't think these kinds of shenanigans were what the Founding Fathers meeting in Philadelphia had in mind.

Writing in the *New Republic*, Franklin Foer chronicles what the *Journal's* Thomas Mooney would consider wholesome political activism. Particularly interesting was Foer's depiction of three topless women wearing gas masks at the rally. Let's hear it for free speech!!!

But more seriously, broadcast accounts of the protest detailed a police raid where law enforcement personnel uncovered protestors conspiring to manufacture Molotov cocktails. For those swept up in the romance of mass demonstrations or who don't know what a Molotov cocktail is, a Molotov cocktail is not something you'll find in Boris Yeltsin's liquor cabinet.

It is an instrument of mayhem where a gasoline-soaked rag is inserted in a glass container to be set on fire and hurled at one's adversaries, usually the police but increasingly private business and property as well. It must be remembered that these are the same people that are usually for unilateral disarmament, gun control, and other assorted pacifist hootenanny.

In his analysis of the World Bank protests, Thomas Mooney is correct in pointing out that such displays are likely to increase in the future. However, such direct action will be no cause of celebration if it is orchestrated in this same kind of lawless manner.

Such displays will in fact testify to the breakdown of traditional American political theory and its replacement by a system of abject nihilism. Concerned citizens would do well to learn about the nature of anrachism as it will come to play a greater role in American life throughout the early years of the 21st century.

While some such as certain trade unionists and pro-sovereignty conservatives spoke out against the World Bank for legitimate reasons, others promoting a far more maniacal agenda merely showed up to stir up trouble. Those doubting such a claim need only research the names of organizations taking part such as "the Ruckus Society" and slogans bandied about such as "Smash the State."

G.K. Chesterton, the English apologist, once remarked that when people no longer believe in God the danger is not that they won't believe in anything but that they will believe in anything. Regarding anarchism, it's not so much that these neo-hippie parasites will fritter their lives away in a nonconstructive manner but that, in their conscientious rejection of all standards and authorities, they will lack the moral wherewithal to withstand any whim or fancy that comes along --- no matter how reprehensible.

In their public relations, many of the more radical elements protesting these institutions of international finance claim to adhere to the principles of nonviolence. However, such promotional literature runs as shallow as the fluff from Madison avenue that these kinds of groups supposedly exist to rail against.

For starters, a number with the movement neglected to inform the general public that they do not see acts of destruction directed at their adversaries as violence. And of the anarchists not prone towards traditional understandings of violence, Franklin Foer writes in the

New Republic, "They might agree that violence is a problem tactically, but they're so steeped in relativism to condemn fellow protestors and too ignorant of ideology to construct a moral case for nonviolence."

Anarchism is here to stay. The goals of this movement do not consist in altering specific policies. Theirs is the total destruction of civilized society. Not only do these hooligans rampage regularly at World Bank summits but they also unleash periodic waves of vandalism in cities scattered across the world each May Day.

Such incidents should belay the myth that Communism no longer exists as a threat to human freedom. It must be noted that, during such escapades in England, a statue honoring Winston Churchill was desecrated with graffiti depicting a hammer and sickle, the nefarious symbol of world Bolshevism.

The World Bank and other institutions of international finance indeed pose a threat to human liberty if these bodies are allowed to usurp American freedoms as elaborated upon in the nation's founding documents such as the Constitution, the Declaration of Independence, and even the Holy Bible.

However, unruly mobs are just as dangerous as their counterparts in planetary administrative bodies since neither extreme of this dispute sees a moral authority higher than themselves. The price of liberty demands eternal vigilance against each of these distinct threats.

Fifth Column Of The Fourth Estate

With tensions increasing between the United States and Russia, it has been noted that the world may be heading into a renewed Cold War. However, such an assertion is not only evident from incidents such as the Hanseen spy case or the expulsion of diplomatic personnel from both countries. The conclusion can also be drawn from the level of ignorance displayed by much of the mainstream media regarding the current international scene and the open hostility of the press to the interests of the United States.

In response to the expulsion of nearly fifty Russian diplomats and other attempts by the Bush Administration to patch the strategic holes in America's tottering ship of state, the *Washington Post* has labeled the President's approach to world affairs as "blunt". The newscast of the local NBC affiliate in Washington labeled Secretary of State Colin Powell's remarks regarding the unnecessary detention of an American University Professor and her preschool-aged son in China as "harsh".

National Security Advisor Condoleezza Rice has provided a perspective more balanced than that offered by rosy-eyed journalists regarding America's adversaries when she was quoted by the March 23, 2001 *Washington Post* as saying, "If we have learned anything in the last several years, it is that a romantic view of Russia --- rather than a realistic one --- did nothing to help the cause of stability in Russia." It hasn't exactly been good for the United States either.

Here are some of the realities liberal journalists are

chastising observant foreign policy experts over for bringing before the public's attention. Instead of aspiring to a level of conduct befitting a place among the brotherhood of upright nations, the actions by Russia and other powers like her would seem to indicate they still reside firmly in the orbit of the darkside.

For example, at the annual World Threat Briefing before the Senate Intelligence Committee in February, it was revealed that both China and Russia plan to deploy measures bent on disrupting U.S. space technology. China, in particular, is developing laser and electronic pulse weapons in pursuit of this objective.

Russia has been equally as busy as well. While Russia and China continue to grow closer through a maniacal partnership directed against the United States, pompous Russian politicians lecture the U.S. as to how a missile defense system designed to protect American citizens from weapons of mass destruction inherently destabilizes the delicate equilibrium of international affairs.

Even regarding this issue, the Russians ply their characteristic deceit and manipulation. Back in February 2001, Russian President Vladimir Putin presented his own proposal for a limited theater-based defense system designed to address the threat of "unpredictable and hostile nations".

While attempting to garnish praise as a world statesman, with such a proposal Putin dances within the shadows of the verbal ambiguities for which those drawn to Communism's allure are famous.

The protection provided to Western nation's by

Putin's plan would be miniscule regarding major threats because Russia would likely not be blacklisted as such a country. Russian and Chinese weapons of mass destruction would continue to possess the opportunity of raining down destruction upon a helpless U.S. population.

Patriotic Americans cannot help but feel a degree of animosity towards nations such as Russia and China for the apocalyptic threat they pose to the United States. Yet each is merely playing its role in the grand geostrategic game all great powers play.

Our deepest contempt ought to be reserved for those among us who actively render ideological aide and intellectual support to the forces actively conspiring to extinguish the light of liberty from this otherwise darkened world.

Almost nowhere is the antipathy towards this nation and the Judeo-Christian heritage it was founded upon as evident as among the media elite. And it must be noted that this disease reaches to the highest levels of mass communications.

Media tycoon Ted Turner recently let his feelings regarding God and country all hang out in a disgusting display of just what his true colors happen to be. Seems he prefers some shade of red.

During his acceptance of an award from the World Federalist Association, he castigated the United States for picking on smaller nations and lavished praise upon the United Nations, claiming we owe our very survival during the Cold War to this global institution. Not one word of gratitude was directed towards the armed forces of the United States in Mr. Turner's remarks nor did he make any acknowledgement of Communism as an inherently flawed system predetermined to failure .

These aspirations for planetary government are often coupled with a hostility towards traditional religious beliefs. Shortly before his comments at the World Federalist Association, Turner smeared his Christian employees by calling them "Jesus freaks."

The World Federalists responded that Turner's comments regarding Christianity were a "moot point". Had these comments been made about Muslims, Jews, or some other ethnic group, old Ted would have not even been in the running for this global governance award.

Ted Turner also told his religious employees at CNN they might prefer working for the Fox News Network, one of Turner's primary competitors. While Fox does have a reputation for producing a news product exhibiting a more refined degree of journalistic objectivity, its corporate echelon has done little more than Turner in the struggle against world Communism. Rupert Murdoch, head of the Fox media empire, might talk a better game, but his actions still fall pitifully short.

According to the March 30, 2001 broadcast of "Point of View with Marlin Maddoux", Murdoch's son gave a speech to a recent business convention. In his comments, the younger Murhdoch argued that the Western media ought not produce stories critical of the regime in China because to do so was unduly antagonistic.

His father has faired little better in standing up to these Marxist thugs. Rupert obsequiously backed down from efforts to market satellite TV to the most populace country on earth because it might destabilize the regime there enslaving around a billion people.

Shows you just how far some will go for the principles embodied by the First Amendment. Seems he has no problem corroding America with programs such as 'Temptation Island" but won't lift a finger to set oppressed nations free with the liberating influence of unfettered information.

Americans face a number of threats from around the globe ranging from acts of terrorism to the proliferation of black-market nuclear weapons to a disturbing resurgence of Communist hostility. The last thing the nation needs is having its primary sources of information in league with or beholden to the enemy at a time when an accurate presentation of the facts is indispensable to our very survival.

Operatives of Obfuscation: Inconsistencies of World Trade/IMF Protestors Second Front Abiding for America's Downfall

A classic maxim teaches that the squeaky wheel gets the grease. Since the Seattle riots of 1999, few wheels have been quite as squeaky as the combustible human detritus that has taken it upon itself to follow international summits around the globe like a pack of rabid wolves.

Political criticism and ethical response must ultimately find justification in a coherent set of principles that bear up to a reasonable degree of analytical scrutiny if such grievances are to be taken seriously by the larger public. And even though this renowned troop of World Trade street thugs might have a knack for smashing windows and ingesting tear gas, any complaints these vagabonds might possess decompose into two-faced ramblings when examined through the criteria of the protestors' own belief systems.

The fundamental inconsistencies between the convictions of these self-professed anarchists and the nature of their grievances were most evident in a incident occurring during a G-8 Summit in Genoa, Italy when a law enforcement officer besieged by marauding hooligans was forced to defend himself by firing his weapon. One demonstrator died as a result.

One traveling troublemaker told the Associated Press at another free-for-all in Frankfurt, Germany that Genoa was a turning point. Other protestors have vowed to step up the violence in response to the audacity of police to defend themselves against injury or attack.

But on what grounds do they justify their complaints and to whom should such criticisms be addressed?

By definition, anarchy is the complete absence of government and law. Anarchism, the application of anarchy as a systematic sociopolitical ideology, is the theory that all forms of government interfere with individual liberty and are therefore undesirable. These, in turn, sprout from the soils of antinomianism, defined by Norman Geisler in *Christian Ethics: Options and Issues* as the ethical belief that there are no objective moral laws.

Protestors assembled at the various international summits have endeavored to implement this worldview on a practical level but cry foul when they befall the consequences of their own ideas. For if there is no right or wrong, frankly what's wrong with the cops cracking a few unruly noggins? And who is it they plan to gripe to when the institutions established to handle the redress of grievances are illegitimate by their own standards?

The Associated Press reported that police threatened jailed Genoan protestors with sexual assault, deprived them of food, and looked on voyeuristically as detainees utilized the toilet facilities.

The hermeneutic of one demonstrator interviewed for the BBC's website on June 18, 2001 might apply to the above situation: "...it's up to each of the people taking part to decide what they do." So if the Italian police get some perverse satisfaction humiliating those in their custody, that's their business. Hey, I'm not for it, but I am one of those stinking moral absolutists impeding so-called social and ethical progress.

This charade of portraying anarchists as care free, live-and-let-live relativists is a sham front used to disguise the movement's far more maniacal nature and intentions. Llewellyn Rockwell, Jr. points out in his essay "The New Communists" that these globetrotting gadabouts are out to destroy capitalism itself. The goal of these anarchists, in their words, is "a new system that would eliminate inequalities between rich and poor, between the powerful and the powerless, and to expand the possibilities of self-determination."

Building a new system would mean abolishing the old. This movement's preferred method for doing so has proven to be what those of us inhibited by reactionary thought patterns usually call violence.

These protestors do not merely employ violence as a

defensive tactic but rather as a tool to impose their will on those around them. On a Fox News special titled "Assignment Danger II" that cataloged the various dangers faced by frontline broadcasters, footage aired of ruffians in Quebec spray-painting mobile news units, hurling hunks of concrete at media equipment, and vocalizing threats of bodily harm directed towards correspondents daring to chronicle these chaotic shenanigans. Fox Reporter Brian Wilson was even forced to defend himself physically against an assault by these rampaging hoodlums.

Rockwell writes, "The attempt [to impose mandatory egalitarianism] would require a looter state on a scale we have not seen since ... the Soviet Union." Rockwell continues, "What life would be like under [such] a regime is foreshadowed in the streets of Genoa: looting, burning, destruction, and chaos."

Thus ultimately, the thing that really has these thugs ticked is being denied the opportunity to impose their own rules and to inflict the brutality themselves. Despite any faults of law enforcement, at least they are bound by and accountable to some objective standard as embodied by law and not unbridled to "do there own thing" as advocated by these slovenly neo-hippies.

Many Americans probably dismiss the beatnik protest movement as a nuisance rather than as a serious threat. However, it's not likely to fritter out with the maturing of these collegians having too much time on their hands.

This propensity towards mayhem and destruction in the name of justice may metastasize into an essential characteristic of the so-called educated mind (i.e. one surrendered to the tripe propagated by the tenured polemicists of perdition). The treatise of treason and terror published by so-called "educators" Michael Hardt and Antonio Negri, Rockwell reports, is so popular as a standard classroom text on American campuses that this rag is often on six week backorder at Harvard University Press. Already it has gained notoriety or infamy (depending on your perspective) as a new *Communist Manifesto*.

The Western World totters along the brink of a destructive revolution determined to destroy all that is good, pure, and holy to be replaced by totalitarian designs devised in the den of the devil himself. Enemies from abroad succeeded in delivering an unbelievable blow to this great nation. We cannot allow grungy rabble from within to finish the job.

A Tale Of Two Rallies

Matthew 7:16-17 says, "Ye shall know them by their fruits... Even so every good tree bringeth forth good fruit; but a corrupt tree bringeth forth evil fruit." Even though various groups gathered in Washington, DC to express their positions regarding a number of issues facing the nation ranging from the Israeli/Palestinian conflict to support (or lack thereof) for the war on terror, these rallies may have proven more instructive in providing the American people with insight into the deportment of these respective activists and how their respective ideologies might manifest themselves in a concrete social situation.

Common themes supposing to link the various

leftist demonstrators descending on the nation's Capital included peace, acceptance, and toleration. You wouldn't have known it from the tone of the rhetoric employed and the behavior displayed at the most prominent protests.

The proverbial center ring of the protests was no doubt the march held in support of the Palestinians, advertised as a stand against war and racism. Someone should have let the participants in on the day's theme.

Had one closed their eyes and merely listened to the ramblings, one would barely been able to distinguish between Klansmen cloaked in white sheets and the unscrubbed beatnik rabble that came to infest some of the nation's most solemn sites during this occasion in terms of the animosity expressed against both Israel and the United States.

According to WorldNetDaily.com, malcontents decried the nation of Israel for "brutalizing" the Palestinian people and even accused the United States of "aiding and abetting Israel to kill Palestinian children." But don't think this crowd was taking a stand against wayward acts of collateral violence or the tangled webs that result from undue foreign involvement. This crowd certainly had little problem with maiming or killing.

This charge cannot be denied by deflecting attention away by labeling the good people at WorldNetDaily as Zionist operatives or whatever the catchy epithet being bantered about this week is to discredit that particular news organization's tireless efforts in exposing the assorted threats arrayed against the United States. The unflinching eye of C-SPAN was also there to dispassionately catalog the unfolding events. Nor have words been put in the mouths of these rabid orators, each instead being incriminated by the content of their own speech.

Sentiments of the assembled were particularly typified by the following chant repeated like a refrain from an irritating chorus: "Long live Palestine! Long live Palestine! We don't care what you say! Intifada all the way!" So much for taking a stand for peace. Apparently the only ones not allowed to protect themselves against violence by a show of force are Israel and the United States.

This alacrity for terrorism was not the result of some naive idealism failing to appreciate the world's current strategic situation. Terrorists, or at least their pompous acolytes, took center stage at the festivities.

Sami Al Arian, a known supporter of Hamas who Bill O'Reilly urged the U.S. intelligence establishment to keep an eye on, told the audience that Israel ought to be given the finger. Others of like-mind urged that the entire Holy Land ought to be surrendered to the Palestinians. So much for eventual coexistence; not one word was raised in opposition to the acts of violence and terror by Islamic extremists more blatantly directed at innocent civilian targets than actions taken by Israeli authorities.

On a lighter note, at least those involved with this demonstration weren't the brightest light bulbs around. One high schooler, who apparently had too much time on her hands and not enough homework since she had organized an activist cell, said the war on terrorism was diverting resources away from education; never mind that defense is a federal matter and education a local concern.

According to WorldNetDaily, Dr. Helen Caldicott (a Nobel Prize nominee no less) likened the Washington Monument to a "phallic symbol" representing the United States as a rogue nation for possessing nuclear weapons. Methinks the caliber of the Nobel pool tis not what it use to be, if it was ever all that to begin with.

And speaking of private bodily organs, that provides a quasi-humorous segway to an equally outrageous display of infantile behavior that occurred at another rally underway at the very same time. Though it did not receive the same amount of attention from the media as those convened by the more obnoxious rabble-rousers, the beleaguered Patriot Rally organized by the upstanding citizens of the Washington, DC chapter of FreeRepublic.com served as a counterdemonstration taking a stand against this confusion and nonsense by supporting both the armed forces of the United States and wholesome American values. As noble as this effort was, its significance did not so much lie in what this group said as in what was done to them.

According to the FreeRepublic account of the event, those opposed to the traditional values expressed by the Patriot Rally did not approach their antagonists in a spirit of dialogue. Instead, these incredibly mature dissidents expressed their disagreement by urinating all over the toilets and bathroom tissue graciously provided by the magnanimous organizers of the Patriot rally.

Park Police also uncovered and foiled a plot by insurgents to overrun these proceedings and to harass the participants engaged in the orderly execution of their Constitutional rights. Park Police also commended the

Freepers as to their orderly conduct in comparison to the leftists who had to be handcuffed and escorted from the premises. But since these hooligans have nothing but contempt for duly constituted authority, I don't imagine those carted off much cared what law enforcement thought.

These situations spawn an interesting array of paradoxes, don't they? On the one hand, these global gadabouts rampage, conniption fit, and destroy property whenever they don't get their way in terms of being allowed to picket anyway they please. Yet on the other, they have no problem with preventing their opponents from exercising the most basic of rights spelled out in America's founding documents such as the Declaration of Independence or the Constitution.

This was particularly evident at the so-called "Die-In", held the Monday after the confabulation honoring Palestinian extremism. At the "Die-In", malcontents ticked-off over U.S. policy in Columbia blocked rush hour traffic by rolling over and playing dead in the middle of the street like a pack of family dogs posturing for attention.

Some might say that these protestors have a right to free expression unhindered by the impositions of decorum and propriety. But what about my right to get to work unimpeded by this hooliganism? Isn't it at least as important? The First Amendment guarantees the right to free speech, not the requirement that others have to pay attention to you. Bet these same ruffians would writhe in disgust if this same tactic was employed by pro-lifers blocking access to an abortion clinic.

Organizers of the "Die-In" told WTOP News Radio that the point of this civil disobedience and social disruption was "to educate commuters and others on how their tax dollars are being used in Colombia." What if I don't care? And what if I don't want to be educated? Employing rhetoric similar to that used by the friends of these people in the abortion movement: my mind, my choice.

But you see, in the mindset of deconstructionist radicalism from which these revolutionary nihilists draw inspiration, fabled rights such as speech, conscience, assembly, and personal determination flow only in one direction. New Left theoretician Herbert Marcuse endorsed this approach through his notion of "repressive tolerance".

The concept of repressive tolerance refuses to grant recognition to the expression of all viewpoints. Rather, this variety of radical tolerance discriminates and excludes, in Marcuse's own words, "movements which are obviously aggressive and destructive", in other words opinions expressed by those with whom Marcuse and like minded associates happen to disagree. That's why these brainless hippies have no problem hooting-down and shouting-out any conservative daring to set foot on campus while crying foul bloody-murder whenever college administrators fail to thank these hellions for looting offices and smashing windows in the name of enlightenment and progressivism.

Under the American political system, these radical protest movements have every right to use the protections of the First Amendment to promote their message. However, they have gone too far when they traverse beyond the boundaries of speech and engage in acts of social disruption or prevent their counterparts from articulating an alternative perspective.

Peace Activists Benefit From Military Action

Three Christian peace activists held by Iraqi insurgents have been rescued by U.S. and British military forces.

Though the story makes clear that the hostages were freed without firing a shot, I don't imagine the soldiers went into a potentially hostile environment unprepared or unprotected.

And that brings us to an interesting point.

If it is the position of these peace activists that it is an abomination before the eyes of God to even have a military or that it is wrong to use force to overcome evil in all instances, shouldn't these prisoners have been willing to remain in the custody of their captors, who are themselves merely adherents of the "religion of peace" responding to the aggression of decadent Western powers, until social workers or other do-gooder types arrived on the scene to negotiate their release through rational persuasion alone?

As with others disposed towards such idealistic nonsense, the inability to defend oneself is an ethical demand to be imposed on everyone else rather than upon those in the vanguard of the revolutionary consciousness.

Opposing specific military actions is one thing. Disavowing the right to fight all together is something else entirely.

These peace activists, refusing to realize the

inherent evil of the terrorist enemy, only have themselves to blame for their frightening ordeal. They should merely thank the Lord that someone would come to their rescue with guns blazing had the need arisen.

Wretched Hive Of Scum & Villainy

Students of political science would be forced to conclude that the field of international relations is a discipline fraught with bizarre irony and stunning contradiction. This is no where as evident as it is at the United Nations.

Both American policymakers and the general public fell victim to this reality in the controversy surrounding the expulsion of the United States from various UN panels such as the Commission on Human Rights and the International Narcotics Control Board.

One almost doesn't know whether to laugh or cry since that these decisions are both a blessing in disguise and a cause for concern all at the same time.

For too long, the United States has drifted along in a state of blissful denial or outright complacency as to the maniacal hootenanny taking place under the auspices of the United Nations.

The United States has been booted off these international bodies largely because of this nation's refusal to submit fully to the yoke of the globalist agenda and for mustering some courage with the advent of the Bush administration to stand up to this planetary nonsense to a limited degree.

It has been speculated that the U.S. is being

punished for challenging UN initiatives regarding issues such as the International Criminal Court, the effort to abolish landmines, and the Kyoto global warming treaty (all of which the United States has rational grounds for opposing).

Yet this dispute between the United States and the United Nations runs deeper than these significant but peripheral policy disputes. These disagreements merely scratch the surface of the ideological chasm festering between these two geopolitical powerhouses.

Increasingly, freedom lovers everywhere find two opposing interpretations as to the nature of human rights competing for prominence in the world at large.

On the one hand can be found the traditional Western view held by the majority of decent upright Americans adhering to the Judeo-Christian worldview that fundamental rights and liberties are granted by God to the individual as an inherent protection against the intrusive tendencies of governments as well as other individuals.

Those holding an opposing standard contend that rights (or rather social privileges) are granted by government and are subject to modification, curtailment, or even outright abolition in pursuit of a regime's particular agenda.

It is this conflict between the differing conceptions of personal liberty that has gotten the United States kicked off the UN panels where the statist interpretation of human rights has come to predominate.

A rundown of the Commission's membership will bear this assertion out. Perusing the Commission's rolls is like taking a tour down Dick Tracy's Rogues Gallery on an international level.

The primary power wanting the U.S. off the Commission was none other than our esteemed "strategic partner" Red China, a nation renowned for its overwhelming devotion to the welfare of the individual. The Communist government there has slaughtered millions in pursuit of dubious ends as epitomized by that county's Great Cultural Revolution. Forced abortions and religious persecution of believing Christians continues in that nation to this very day.

Another paragon of inalienable rights guiding the Commission to ever higher plateaus of individual emancipation is Saudi Arabia. In that particular land of opportunity, women aren't even allowed to drive cars and those who convert from Islam to another faith are rewarded by having their heads lopped off.

One will realize just how ludicrous the decision to remove the United States from the Commission really is once they learn that the seat belonging to the beacon of hope to the world in this life was given to Sudan. Thus a nation where children are sold into the bondage of slavery for simply belonging to the "wrong" religion has been elevated as a better example to the world than the land of the free and the home of the brave.

Even the more enlightened and civilized nations on the Human Rights Commission leave something to be desired in their interpretation of fundamental rights and liberties.

For example, in Canada one can run afoul of the law for speaking out against homosexuality and a number of Evangelicals have been subject to criminal prosecution there for distributing literature critical of other religions. Other industrialized democracies on the Human Rights Commission such as France, Germany, and even the United Kingdom have laws unduly hampering religious and individual expression.

A number of those opposed to the controversial agenda being pursued by the United Nations have suggested that now is the perfect time to get out of this planetary bureaucracy in light of this slap across the face of the United States since the UN largely pursues an anti-American agenda at the expense of U.S. taxpayers.

Rather it is the time to rally goodhearted people to the side of our cause rather than to run from the fight. Edmund Burke is credited with saying that all it takes for evil to win is for good men to do nothing.

The only thing protecting the people of the world from the full wrath of the diabolical intentions of the United Nations is the love of freedom and concern for justice found at the heart of the American spirit. Without this influence, such evil would know no bounds.

Without an American presence to temper its decisions, the Human Rights Commission has continued its downward spiral of propagating policies inimical to a true understanding of human rights.

Soon after banishing the United States, the Commission proceeded to bar nongovernmental organizations such as the Family Research Council and the Simon Weisenthal Center from providing input regarding the work of the Commission because of the practice of these associations to speak out against atrocities around the world.

According to the May 17, 2001 *Washington Times,* it is becoming increasingly difficult for such watchdog organizations to get the bureaucratic clearance necessary to participate in UN forums and meetings. Joanna Weschler of Human Rights Watch pointed out in the article that repressive governments have been emboldened to deny the right of petition to organizations opposed to the totalitarian style of administration since Sudan successfully banished the abolitionist Christian Solidarity International from participating at UN functions.

Unless America stands its ground, things will only get worse. According to the radio news program "Point of View with Marlin Maddoux", UN "peacekeepers" in Sudan threatened to use helicopter gunships on missionaries trying to deliver Bibles to Christian refuges in that beleaguered country. Perhaps such military force should be brought to bear against Sudan's radical Islamic government when that regime decides to drop bombs as it has done in the past on Samaritan's Purse hospitals, the relief organization administered by Billy Graham's son Franklin.

These outrages are nothing compared to what the UN has in store for the world in general and America in particular if the institution could ever avail itself of such an opportunity.

For example, it is the ultimate goal of the United Nations to establish an independent standing army financed through taxation extracted from all international commercial transactions. And with the threat of force, even nations who might otherwise oppose such globalist nonsense could eventually be forced to comply or face military occupation, with their citizens subject to the same kinds of laws governing the most brutal nations on earth.

It is therefore imperative for the United States to remain active within the United Nations for the time being if for no other reason than to try and hold this Hobbesian leviathan at bay along with its proposals of perdition.

It would do good indeed for the United States to disentangle itself from the snares set by these world bodies whose intentions stretch far beyond the aversion of global war and the maintenance of amicable relations between nations. However, the United States must not leave the table with its back turned to such a den of cutthroats and vipers. The United States, not the United Nations, must be the last one standing on the world stage in reference to this planetary showdown.

In the movie *Star Wars*, immediately prior to entering the scene in the sleazy bar Obi-Wan Kenobi says, "You'll never find a more wretched hive of scum and villainy. We must be cautious." Such words of wisdom are quite apropos regarding America's relationship to the United Nations.

The UN's Diabolical Agenda

At the Millennium Summit, those gathered to celebrate the 55th anniversary of the United Nations did not assemble to nibble cake and sip champagne. Rather, delegates and world leaders convened at the gathering to set the ball rolling toward the next level of global administration.

In the minds of most Americans, the purpose of the

UN is to prevent the likelihood of a catastrophic war by serving as a forum where conflicting parties can assemble to discuss their differences. An examination of the UN's true aspirations would cause such a rosy image to evaporate like a drop of water on a parched summer day.

For if Americans think they have it bad now under the current U.S. tax system, they haven't seen anything until the one being proposed by the UN is implemented. Under the proposal, forms of international commerce such as airline tickets and the transport of goods would be subject to taxation.

However, these funds would not go for the upkeep of international infrastructure alone. The primary purpose of this revenue system would be to fund a global welfare scheme designed to redistribute resources from wealthier nations to the poorer ones.

Despite these ambitions, it is not enough to occupy the minds of those conspiring to rule the world.

Prior to the Millennium Summit, another summit was convened among world religious leaders to discuss the role they would play in the onward march to the New World Order. Instead of serving as a forum in which to discuss the ways religion could be used to patch the world's deteriorating moral climate, those running this pagan powwow such as Ted Turner and similar theological heavyweights used it as a sledgehammer to bash Evangelicals, Catholics, and even Muslims daring to stand in opposition to the UN's promotion of homosexuality, legalized prostitution, and other related measures deleterious to individual character and the integrity of the family.

Those thinking America's power and prestige will protect them from this stupidity of global proportions are in for an even ruder awakening.

For decades, American leaders of both parties have bent over backwards in praise of the rush towards planetary government. But even if America somehow mustered the courage to stand against this formidable tide, the U.S. could be forced to handover its nuclear deterrent or face the wrath of a proposed UN army. There will be little the American people would be able to do to protect themselves and their families from rape and pillage by the forces of less civilized nations such as Russia, Red China, and the remainder of the Third World since global gun control is yet another item to be found on the robust policy platter set before the United Nations.

But perhaps the saddest thing of all, even beyond the bleak future being planned for the United States, is the fact that the media (the institution charged with warning the American people as to the nature of the threats arrayed against the nation's liberty) thinks it is more important to inform the American people as to the occasional profanity that falls form the President's or Vice President's lips or of Bush's shortcomings in pronouncing the word "subliminal", a linguistic mouthful few of us could wrap our tongues around.

If the American people do not soon awaken to this threat of apocalyptic proportions, in all likelihood America as we know it will cease to exist, with our freedom and our godly heritage subordinated to a global leviathan that cares little for either.

UN Proposal A Threat To U.S.

Faced with a dizzying array of laws, statutes and bureaucratic regulations, many Americans are afraid to speak to the youngsters across the street for fear of one day being charged with child abuse or swat a pesky bug buzzing around their ear for fear of violating endangered species protections. Americans may soon find themselves subject to yet another layer of judicial control and bureaucratic intervention.

The United Nations has established the International Criminal Court, modeled after the war crimes tribunals following World War II, to prosecute atrocities such as those committed by the Nazis and more recently such as those in Yugoslavia.

In this era of nuclear proliferation, biochemical warfare and international terrorism, who could possibly oppose such an institution designed to address these horrors evoking fear from any rational human being? Fortunately, in the United States cooler heads have prevailed for now and the treaty has not been ratified.

However, it yet remains to be seen how American citizens will be protected from the most disturbing clauses of this global agreement. Contained within the treaty is a provision that would allow the court to arrest and indict U.S. citizens for violations of international law.

Many will no doubt dismiss such concerns, thinking that only terrorists, dope peddlers, and other kinds of international ne'er-do-wells need fear this global judicial body. Such apathy may quickly evaporate upon learning what exactly might constitute a crime under the auspices of the United Nations. One might discover that known terrorists and their sympathizers such as Yasir Arafat and Osama Bin Ladin could fair better than the average American.

For while the United Nations might have a role to play as a policy forum whereby conflicting nations can air their differences in hopes of avoiding catastrophic violence, the institution has strayed on a number of occasions into matters best addressed by other existing policy mechanisms.

Typifying the intrusive darker side of the UN is the organization's convention regarding the rights of children. This document forbids corporeal punishment, compulsory religious instruction from parents, and efforts to block a minor's access to news information. In plain English, in the eyes of the United Nations, being a decent parent puts one in the same league as Osama Bin Ladin.

What is to stop the court from exercising its jurisdiction in these matters? Apparently nothing, as the *Washington Times* reported that opponents in the Senate voted the treaty down since it lacked clauses protecting Americans from frivolous or ideologically motivated prosecutions.

Vigilance must continue to be exercised in regards to this issue given the anti-American inclinations of those favorable to the UN social agenda. Racial agitators such as Louis Farakhan and Jesse Jackson have in the past petitioned the United Nations to intervene in American domestic affairs in order to correct alleged racial injustices. The reader should be reminded that radical pluralists have often argued that anyone daring to declare one religion as the sole source of truth comes dangerously close to enunciating hate speech, which is often a crime in many so-called "social democracies".

History teaches that laws emanating from the legislative source farthest from the individual are often the most tyrannical. How much more so when the laws in question and the means used to enforce them are found beyond the pillars upon which our liberties rest?

Failure Of Treaty Good For America

Sometimes the principles of international affairs seemingly defy logic on first view but ring with an undeniable truth upon further reflection.

For example, if a nation desires peace, it must prepare for war. Another such truism teaches that the adversaries of this great nation hide behind the most eloquent precepts in order to cloak their own ignominious machinations.

In 1999, the U.S. Senate voted not to ratify the Comprehensive Nuclear Test Ban Treaty. This decision sparked considerable debate throughout the world community, especially among those not known for their fidelity to the ideals of human well-being.

The Russian Foreign Ministry issued a statement chastising the United States for endangering international stability. As if Russia has any room to talk in regards to these kinds of matters.

It must be remembered that, under the banner of the former Soviet Union, the Russian government fomented violent revolution around the globe in the form of terrorism and other violent acts such as those precipitating the Cuban Missile Crisis. Russia is still perhaps one of the greatest sources of geopolitical destabilization in the world today as former Communists mutate into mafia kingpins selling weapons of mass destruction to the highest bidders.

China also expressed its own "profound regret" at U.S. refusal to ratify the treaty.

The only thing China regrets is that there are still a few American statesman stalwart enough not to have the wool pulled over their eyes, unlike Traitor-In-Chief Bill Clinton who allowed the Red Chinese to acquire U.S. nuclear technology obtained in exchange for underhanded campaign contributions. One is forced to wonder if these highly principled Maoists will forego implementing the technology through surreptitious means for the sake of international brotherhood.

Contrary to multiculturalists and internationalists, not all of those running the nations of the world abide by the same high standards by which the United States operates. As the pinnacle of goodness in the world, America must protect itself against maniacal regimes, despots, and radicals bent on destroying our own cherished way of life since it stands in stark contrast to their own totalitarian worldviews.

Those opposed to the Comprehensive Test Ban Treaty pointed out that the treaty is unverifiable and could ultimately compromise the reliability of the nation's nuclear deterrent. Is anyone really so naive to believe that individuals such as Saddam Hussein having records of going out of their way to flout the standards of civilized conduct will abide by such an agreement?

And even if agreements could be enforced, such restrictions would be strategically questionable because of the pressure they impose upon the concept of national sovereignty. After all, do we really want the Russians or the Red Chinese having final authority over America's most crucial defensive policies and operations?

The realm of international politics is a realm governed by the laws of the playground where the only thing stopping the bully from beating someone up is the realization that the intended victim may be capable of inflicting equal or greater harm in return.

The Associated Press quoted the Mayor of Hiroshima as saying, "The U.S. should lead the way to end the proliferation of nuclear weapons." The only thing the United States has to do is protect its citizens, its territory, and its interests from the threats to life and liberty loose in the world today.

Clinton Stance On Pregnant Chinese Refuges Shameful

The very same Clinton Administration claming itself the champion of "women's rights" plans to deport several female Chinese refuges who fled their Communist homeland fearing forced abortions and sterilizations.

Some might contend that as a sovereign nation it is the right of the United States government to determine admittance criteria. However, it should be noted that the immigration and political asylum process has already degenerated into a mockery of the American system of due process and bureaucratic procedure.

For example, liberals want to add to the mix of those demanding special entrance status a new class known as economic refuges whose only claim to sympathy is having lived in dire poverty, which is the plight of about 75% of those hailing from the Third World. They would add this to the present situation where refuges show up claiming political persecution only to jump ship on their administrative hearing dates into the anonymous fabric of metropolitan American life. Yet President Clinton would have had us believe a handful of Chinese women would sink the ship of state.

Such a policy reveals that Clinton is not an ardent defender of women's rights as he is of abortion. Liberals of his ilk often purport that it is the right of the woman to determine the fate of her womb's contents. Those being anesthetized and pried open like a change purse by Communist hordes while strapped to a cold metal slab aren't exactly giving their consent under contemporary contract law.

If the American government wants to maintain the right of choice, isn't it forced to defend the rights of women to keep their offspring? After all, liberals speak against the pro-life policies of Ireland and would surely grant sanctuary to an Iranian woman seeking an abortion in violation of the Islamic tenets of her fundamentalist homeland.

But despite the excuses and grandiose policy proclamations put forward to justify the Clinton position, in the end it all boils down to the fact that the freedom of choice is little more than a license to kill.

Underneath The Turban of Deceit

Though America's Islamic adversaries might claim to be fighting for their own values in their own way, truth and fairness obviously fail to rank high among them. For while Islamic activists dare anyone to speak ill of their cherished faith, it seems they have no intentions of bestowing the same pluralistic courtesies they expect for themselves upon their American, Christian, or Jewish counterparts.

On "The 700 Club", Pat Robertson went into a detailed analysis regarding the Islamic challenge facing the United States. In his comments, Robertson classified Islam (in the words of the *Washington Post)* as a "violent religion bent on world domination".

Both multiculturalists and Islamic interest groups immediately responded in protest, with a *Washington Post* editorial labeling Robertson's comments "the least appropriate public statement by any prominent citizen since Sept 11". Never mind the fact there could have been a considerable degree of truth to what Brother Robertson had to say.

For while it would be irresponsible to hold all individual Muslims personally responsible for the September 11th attack, vocal adherents of this particular religion have expressed such a virulent and widespread antipathy towards the United States that discerning citizens cannot help but exhibit a healthy suspicion of those representing this competing civilization. These warning signs extend from ideological posturing, to political mobilization, to outright threats and violence.

Hussein Ibish of the Arab American Anti-Discrimination Committee told the *Washington Post* that Robertson's comments that Islam is not a peaceful religion were outrageous. More likely Mr. Ibish is the one trying to pull the wool over the eyes of the American people.

The very same *Washington Post* that lamented Pat Robertson's comments in its February 24, 2002 editorial ran a story the very next day examining the role and nature of the Islamic academies popping up around the country. But in these particular halls of scholarship, readers might be surprised to learn that the three "R's" instead stand for "reading", "writing", and "revolution."

Most American citizens would no doubt pay little heed to these schools, overlooking them as innocuous examples of America's vibrant tradition of private education. However, most schools in this particular sector of the scholastic economy don't teach the kinds of things being propagated in some of these Islamic academies.

According to the *Washington Post*, one textbook used at one of these schools contained the following: "Oh Musilm, here is a Jew... Come here and kill him." And this is the mild stuff. The really juicy material can be found in some of the mosques scattered across the United States and Europe.

Most houses of worship taking their respective beliefs seriously provide access to assorted print, audio, and video resources that augment their teaching activities and support their most cherished doctrines. While most Christian churches posses works on Sunday school administration, Biblical interpretation and missionary biographies, the publications found among the collections of these parallel Islamic institutions tend to be more rambunctious regarding the subject material they address.

An article appearing in the March 3, 2002 *Washington Post* provides an enlightening review of the bibliographic selections available on the shelves of one British mosque in particular. One book is entitled *A Beginner's Guide to Unarmed Combat;* the title pretty much says it all. Related videos teach viewers how to break limbs, twist arms and slit throats. Gives a whole new meaning to spiritual warfare doesn't it?

Such literature serves a purpose beyond a leisurely afternoon's light reading. For while Evangelical Christians squabble as to whether or not they should even acknowledge the existence of social issues having religious implications, Islam possess no such qualms as it is a faith quite open about its aspirations of making the world submit to Allah on bended knee.

Having brought much of the Middle East, along with parts of Africa and Asia, under their control, Muslim zealots have now turned their eyes towards a prize they have not had within their grasp since the late Middle Ages or Early Modern period --- the lucrative lands of the infidel West.

For while Muslims in America expect Christians to keep their religion to themselves and out of the public square, politically active Muslims don't think such a prohibition should apply to themselves. This is where observers of socio-religious activity uncover a disturbing intermingling between those of this particular faith who purport to work within the legitimate framework of a democratic republic and those who insist upon winning their political way through means of violence.

In February 2002, WorldNetDaily.com profiled organizations straddling the fence between playing within the rules and backing those out to destroy the system in which the rules of legitimacy exist. The article noted that the Council on American-Islamic Relations sports an apple pie image by sponsoring otherwise wholesome activities such as voter registration drives yet at the same time lends support to purveyors of destruction, mayhem, and death such as Hamas and Islamic Jihad.

Renowned terrorism expert Steve Emerson told WorldNetDaily, "They may not admit it, but ultimately they want to make the U.S. a Muslim country. In the interim, they want to acquire as much political power as possible to push their agenda to be afforded legitimacy by political officials."

For his efforts to expose this threat to the United States, The Council on American-Islamic relations labeled Emerson "the attack dog of the extremist wing of America's pro-Israel lobby." Just ask Salman Rushdie what happens to those who say similar things about Islam. Like Mr. Rushdie, Mr. Emerson must also take extraordinary precautions to protect his own life.

Note, though, Steve Emerson's claims have not been refuted and in fact are borne out by the positions taken by Muslim leaders themselves. Pastor John Hagee of Cornerstone Church in San Antonio, Texas in a sermon on Islam noted that the first Islamic chaplain to open the United States Congress in prayer later went on to enunciate his desire to abolish the Constitution and replace it with an Islamic system of government.

President Bush has repeatedly insisted that America view Islam as a peaceful religion. However, that task is exceedingly difficult when the foremost leaders of that particular religion paraded before the people of the United States make statements indicating otherwise.

For example, that little Muslim cleric who addressed the memorial service at the National Cathedral in Washington commemorating the September attacks was later revealed to have publicized his support for Hamas. WorldNetDaily quotes Abdulbrahman Alamoudi of the American Muslim Council as saying, "I have been labeled ... a supporter of Hamas. We are all supporters of Hamas. I wish they added that I am also a supporter of Hezbollah."

Should Islamists ever come to power in this country, one can be assured they will have no intention of continuing America's system of traditional freedoms and liberties if other Islamic regimes around the world are to serve as models of what members of this particular religion might achieve here employing similar ideologies and belief systems.

Phillip Zodhiates, in an email letter circulated under the auspices of Christianpetitions.com, highlights *Wall Street Journal* statistics that all but one of the world's remaining military regimes are Islamic, that 28 of the 30 active conflicts around the world involve Islamic parties, and that two-thirds of the worlds political prisoners languish in Islamic prisons. Hardly any Islamic nations hold meaningful elections satisfactory to Western standards.

Citizens troubled by the increasing influence of Islam in our society must walk a fine line. After all, there are many liberal secularists raising an even bigger fuss over private Christian education and political participation. Having been admitted into the midst of American society, Muslims cannot be denied access to these coveted venues of public discourse unless their actions directly threaten innocent lives. Likewise, it is appropriate, however, for the rest of us to use these same constitutional forms of speech to question the peculiarity and appropriateness of the nation's newest arrivals expressing the most vitriolic disdain for this great nation when no one forced them to migrate to a place they so claim to despise and seek to destroy.

A Terrorist by Any Other Name

In response to the September 11th Attack upon America, the U.S. government has vowed to wipe terrorism from the face of the earth. To some officials, this noble struggle might become nothing more than a word game of shuffled papers and fluctuating definitions.

Before the advent of Osama Bin Ladin, Libyan dictator Muammar Qaddafi spent several decades atop terrorism's hit parade. However, if some within the State Department have their way, transgressions against the United States such as the Lockerbie Bombing will become little more than an unfortunate misunderstanding (provided Qaddafi coughs up $6 billion in compensation).

These terms are being offered, it is argued, because Libya has supposedly not sponsored anti-American terrorism in over ten years and has cooperated in the campaign against Osama Bin Ladin.

Little Muammar might be putting up a better front; but evidence indicates he has merely altered tactics, not his underlying modus operandi.

In his effort to establish an African version of the European Common Market, Qaddafi has called for the expulsion of all Whites from the Dark Continent. This is more than idol rhetoric. Whites in countries such as Zimbabwe and South Africa have been attacked by marauding hooligans with little protection from their respective governments.

Intelligence reports also indicate Libya has built a massive underground complex in all likelihood dedicated to the development of weapons of mass destruction. Of course, this could be just another aspirin factory.

Just because Qaddafi operatives aren't currently flying airplanes into skyscrapers does not make him any less dangerous than Osama Bin Ladin. Perhaps he is even more so as officials charged with protecting America from the kind of threat the Colonel represents seem once again content to ignore the warning signals emanating from that tumultuous part of the world.

Bombers Disguise Themselves As Women

I've discussed this before among colleagues and associates as to the propriety of Muslims retaining the trappings of their traditional garb and head-coverings.

Suicide bombers disguised as women have blown up an Iraqi mosque, killing 79 and wounding over 100.

While Muslim women are to be commended for dressing modestly as modernized women continue to dress sluttier and sluttier with piercings through their navels and tattoos scrawled across their backs jiggling out there in the open for all the world to see, Western societies need to think long and hard about allowing additional immigrants from lands where this mode of dress is prevalent to settle in industrialized nations.

At the very least, bans on face veils should be considered because when their mugs are concealed you don't know whether there's a good looking dame under there or a pile of whiskers out to blow you up.

Americans would not tolerant Klansmen going about unimpeded with their faces concealed. Then why allow it by those practicing an interpretation of a particular world faith just as dedicated to implementing their pernicious ideology through any means necessary?

Was Russian School Massacre A Preview Of Things To Come?

The tragic siege of the school in Russia has come to an end, but its horror will continue to reverberate for weeks and maybe even years to come.

For even though the Russian people bear the brunt of this unjustifiable assault, it also serves as a warning to the United States and any other world power standing in opposition to the barbarity of modern terrorism.

Though the incident is portrayed as one of Chechen separatism and independence, buried in various news accounts is the tidbit that Arabs were also discovered to be part of the operation. Such mercenaries could very well be

Al Qaeda.

Since the attack on the train in Spain is believed to have been a rehearsal for a future election season attack upon the U.S., this new tactic of targeting school children doesn't bode well for civilized nations.

Discerning Americans are forced to ask how long until rabid sandmonkeys pull a stunt like this here. Terrorists could very well hold a school here hostage and threaten to harm the pupils should voters reelect President Bush to public office.

When it happens, one can only hope liberals will realize just how useless tolerance, multiculturalism and open borders are in dealing with those who make children drink their own urine as transpired during the siege at the Russian school.

Sadly, such a tragedy would probably be the only thing that might disimbue these naive progressives of their misguided view of the world. After all, it has been said that a liberal is a conservative that hasn't been mugged yet.

Having to pick between unspeakable tragedies, too bad such a jarring lesson couldn't be taught during one of those antiwar protest rallies instead of snuffing out the lives of innocent children who've yet to take any kind of position whatsoever in regards to current world conflicts.

Reaction To Saddam Centerfold Exposes Moral Bankruptcy Of Islamist Sympathizers

Media leftists are decrying pictures of Saddam in his BVD's. They insist such treatment is a testament to the lechery of the West and supposedly brutal tactics used by his captors.

But in reality, the response tells us more about those doing the complaining than about the incarceration policies of the U.S. military.

While most of us would be embarrassed if pictures of ourselves in our knickers made it into the local paper, we need to remember for just a second who Saddam Hussein is and the lifestyle that he has led.

American-hating liberals and their pet savages in the Middle East expect us to have sympathy for this hemorrhoid on the rear-end of humanity that hacked apart his enemies, shipped them back in little bags to their families, and expected to be paid for doing them the favor. To prisoners under his regime, having their pictures taken in their undies would have been a good day.

If anything, Saddam's calendar layout should be seen as proof as to the beneficence of his caretakers. The cameras (as we are told of those cataloging our every move) are there for his own good.

If the devotees of tyranny and terror prefer, we can always have the cameras removed. Then if we're lucky, Saddam will do us a favor and pull a Heinrich Himmler or Herman Goerring.

At the end of World War II, Adolf Hitler committed suicide in part out of fear of being put on public display. Today it seems the gullibility of the viewing public could be the caged dictator's best friend.

If Earl Had To Die, Why Not Saddam?

Moral relativism contends that principles change depending upon the situation. It also becomes a convenient tool by which to justify politically correct causes while condemning others for pursuing courses of action one does not agree with.

This cognitive discontinuity has come into particular focus in regards to the sentiments expressed by celebrities in reference to the selective application of force or violence. These pampered dolts make careers of glamorizing it when it arises in inappropriate (though fictionalized) contexts but get more sanctimonious than Dana Carvey's "Saturday Night Live's" Church Lady upon catching wind that a robust but unfortunate physical response is necessary to protect the innocent, uphold justice, and preserve liberty here in the real world. Fortunately for us, most of these dilettantes aren't known for being profound thinkers, but they must be countered before what they pass off as reason infects too many minds.

In the Dixie Chicks' ditty "Goodbye Earl" an abused wife and her friend conspire to kill her wretch of a husband and ultimately carry through with the plan. In the real world, the group's lead singer told a London audience that the trio was ashamed President Bush was from Texas.

These shrill banshees compounded their verbal outrage by justifying the earlier comments in light of "the anti-American sentiment that has unfolded here [in Europe which] is astounding." These profound geopolitical strategists continued, "...the president is ignoring the opinion of many in the U.S. and alienating the rest of the world."

So to these discordant floozies, popularity is the sole criteria by which deadly force is determined to be right or wrong. But in the final analysis, Saddam deserves to die a whole lot more than Earl ever did.

In "Goodbye Earl", the distraught wife decides on her particular course of action because of the law's failure to prevent Earl from inflicting considerable bodily harm upon her. Likewise, President Bush has been forced to take action in Iraq because of the failure and incapability of the international system to coax cooperation through collegial persuasion. But unlike the protagonists (for lack of a better term) in the song, at least President Bush is justified in his actions.

This homicide on the part of Mary Anne and Wanda boils down to mere revenge. Horrible as Earl was in the song, he was not whacked off in self-defense during one of his frequent rampages. He was the victim of tainted black eye peas, meaning aforethought was involved.

"So what?" you may ask, "He got what he deserved." Perhaps, but would feminists, social workers, and all-around-man-haters feel the same way if the politically incorrect shoe was on the other foot and an abused husband (yes, there are husbands physically abused by their wives a "20/20" report admitted) premeditatedly did away with his spouse?

Apparently the proto-Marxian distinctions of contemporary victimology are all that matter to the Dixie Chicks, so much so they would deny the right to protect oneself to those falling outside the parameters of their progressivist paradigms. For unlike the glorified scoundrels in this ballad, the actions taken by President Bush and the armed forces of the United States are most appropriate.

Some might counter that, like the characters in the song, President Bush is merely seeking revenge. That is an incorrect analogy.

The current operation in Iraq has more in common with an act of self-defense. The threat of weapons of mass destruction and other assorted forms of terrorism are the metaphysical equivalent of a cocked gun being pointed at the head of the United States.

Would the Dixie Chicks and the spineless peaceniks suggest nothing be done to ameliorate this danger? Will they feel the same way should members of their families become victims of the next attack, or even fall victims themselves, ironically, during one of their own self-absorbed rallies or concerts? One might easily muse that a protestor is simply someone who has not been nuked yet.

In other less-subversive (but equally uninformed circles), Americans are hearing the typically misapplied axioms about the need to turn the other cheek and such. But where these kinds of weapons are concerned, should the enemies of Christendom be allowed to land the first blow, there won't be much of a cheek left to turn as both of them will have been blown away by the searing energy of the split atom or festered over with oozing sores from the stench-ridden puss of some nightmarish pestilence.

Distinction must also be made between the status of those in the song and U.S. armed forces. Projecting Mary

Anne and Wanda onto the world stage would mean a bunch of self-appointed yahoos addressed the Iraqi menace by getting in their pickups and driving to Baghdad to beat the stuffings out of Hussein.

Sending in the military is more akin to calling the police, meaning there are certain spheres of authority designed to address these kinds of misfortunes in specific contexts. Faced with imminent harm at a given instant, it is proper for the individual to do whatever is necessary to neutralize the threat; removed from the danger by the passage of time, it becomes the duty of other constituted authorities to oversee and possibly administer any necessary redress of grievances.

Ironically though, both Earl and Saddam have quite a bit in common, with Saddam and his cronies outranking this petty wife beater along the continuum of evil. Saddam's son Uday tortured and executed members of the Iraqi soccer team, tossed dissidents into recycling shredders, and raped at leisure any woman happening to catch his fiendish eye.

One would think these pinko feminists would rally to the cause to oust these unmannered monsters. After all, these are the same kinds of agitators that rose up in umbrage against Clarence Thomas whose only mistake was not marrying Anita Hill after daring to flirt with that old bat.

But perhaps worse than the inconsistent positions espoused by the Dixie Chicks is the attitude in which they are expressed. In the video, the Chicks cavort gingerly before the camera with the actor portraying Earl's corpse joyously joining in. The Administration, on the other hand, has overall approached the war with the utmost seriousness. Who do I ask you, dear friends, lacks respect for human life: three hussies who celebrate blatant murder with ecstatic glee or a President who looks like he has the weight of the world bearing-down on his shoulders each and every time he informs the American people of what must be done to defend this great land?

Right Not To Listen

The laws of physics teach that for every action there is an equal and opposite reaction. Something similar could be said in the realm of political thought as many traditional rights can be exercised in an almost Taoist fashion, meaning they can be actively or passively employed. For example, one enjoys the benefits of the Second Amendment whether one becomes an enthusiastic sharpshooter or abstains from firearms totally as an avid pacifist.

Yet certain liberals aren't likely to admit that the First Amendment is itself also a two-way street. But if you are free to say what you want, then it follows I am just as much within my rights not to listen.

In his response to my criticism of the Dixie Chicks, Mike Sarzo at PolitixGroup.com reveals what the average liberal believes regarding free expression and to whom it should be granted. As with most other aspects of this ideology, its positions regarding these issues are an opaque montage of twisted logic imperiling both commonsense and human liberty.

Sarzo writes, "One aspect of freedom of speech is

that it often covers speech that you don't agree with, ... the right also covers your freedom to say something even if everyone else doesn't agree with you." Funny, he opened his essay saying, "Frederick Meekins' recent column berating the Dixie Chicks was a poorly worded, badly reasoned set of grade school-styled barbs that have no place on a website of political debate."

In other words, political discourse should be as about as stimulating as hearing Al Gore recite the alphabet. So much for celebrating opinions with which ones does not agree. Seems such lofty platitudes are nullified if you happen to disagree with Mr. Sarzo.

No where did I say that the Dixie Chicks should have their constitutional rights abridged. That said, that does not mean we cannot use our own speech to criticize those we deem to be utilizing this sacred trust inappropriately or refuse to lavish them with the bounty of unfettered commerce for enunciating values antithetical to our own worldview.

But apart from questioning my nearly infallible intellect, the danger of those like Mike Sarzo arise in their propensity to view rights in a relativistic utilitarian sense rather than in an inalienable absolutist manner. For if thinkers view rights as descending from an alterable, finite source such as government or culture, then these precepts can be manipulated to suit whatever elite happens to be pulling the strings.

Mike Sarzo bemoans anyone daring to question the anti-American rabble, but has little concern about denying these same rights to the more-backwards people of the earth. Moral absolutists, on the other hand, hold that, as individual human beings, all men are created equal; however, their respective cultures are not. Some ways of life are inherently superior to others.

Sarzo writes, "For better or worse, many throughout the world are not culturally inclined to support the idea of having a system that mirrors the American system of government... To assume that most people want or need democracy is ... yet another example of [the] provincialism that has contributed to much anti-American resentment throughout the world." I guess this overwhelming disgust for at least the material component of our way of life is why our metropolitan areas are so packed with immigrants now that many of these areas no longer resemble America anymore.

According to Mike Sarzo, some people don't deserve to be free in their native lands. Perhaps he sees nothing wrong with Uday grabbing woman off the street to rape for his own sadistic pleasure. Those who languished under Saddam's iron rule had far more serious abridgements of fundamental freedoms to worry about than whether or not their albums would remain atop the Billboard charts.

Mr. Sarzo hems and haws about the shortsightedness of provincialism but himself fails to comprehend basic geopolitical strategy. Sure, there might be regimes that posed a more direct threat to the United States than Hussein's Iraq as Sarzo claims; but when cleaning house, you've got to start somewhere.

Apart from the defensive value of eliminating (or at least crippling) a major bastion and fomenter of world terrorism, Iraq was selected in part to serve as an example as to what awaits the rogues, tyrants, and all-around scumbags daring to kindle America's righteous indignation. For the most part, the U.S. can only take on so many adversaries at one time.

It is, therefore, prudent first to topple those nations already tottering on the brink of collapse. Once Iraq is squared away, the U.S. should prepare to put Syria and Iran in their places if they don't come to their senses. We'll even take on the French if we have to; I am sure the Boy Scouts will enjoy the snail-eaters cowering before them.

Islam has been around for over a thousand years. Terrorism won't be going away over night. These things will take time.

Part of the justification for this ongoing war against terrorism is the preservation of the basic liberties that make America a shining beacon to freedom-loving people all around the world. The right to express dissention must be upheld. Likewise, my right to ignore such inane prattle by refusing to listen or to reward you is just as essential to the continuance of this grand republic.

Eurosnobbery:
Declining Third-Rate Nations Ought Mind
Their Own Decaying Cultures

It has become fashionable liberal parlance to criticize the tendency of the American people to promote their way as the right way. Yet in light of the reaction by some of the nations most prone to caste aspersion over the McVeigh execution, it would seem these countries normally priding themselves on the detached moral tolerance characterizing their own cultures ought to abide by their own advice.

Despising the conservative leanings in the policy agenda espoused by the Bush administration, European elitists are using the McVeigh execution as an excuse, as well as differences over issues such as global warming and strategic missile defense, to defame America's image in the eyes of the world.

Amnesty International is quoted in a Reuters story as saying, "By executing the first federal death row prisoner in nearly four decades, the US has allowed vengeance to triumph over justice and distance itself yet further from the aspirations of the world community." The Portuguese human rights group Law and Justice added to this sentiment by saying, "The death penalty is a barbarism inappropriate to our times." Hooligans across Europe have taken to the streets in protest of both President Bush and the McVeigh execution.

Yet it must be remembered that these are the same European powers who played a role in orchestrating the removal of the United States from the UN Commission on Human Rights and its replacement with Sudan. These countries also don't seem to have a problem with conducting normalized relations with known sponsors of terrorism and oppression such as Iran and Cuba.

The people of the world should not be lulled into thinking that Europe has done much recently for the cause of human rights and freedom around the globe. For these very same countries thinking one should be able to blow apart over 168 people and to ruin the lives of countless others without a similar degree of misery being inflicted upon the perpetrator themselves go out of their way to curtail more traditional conceptions of individual liberty.

If anything, European governments have become something of an impediment in this particular arena of social undertaking. One time, I wrote on an Italian proposal that would have outlawed the criticism of homosexuality in that country. Now the French have enacted an equally disturbing piece of legislation.

For while the United States gets roundly hooted-down for anesthetizing one of the most loathsome criminals to mar the landscape of the twentieth century, the French government threatens to imprison for up to five years or fine up to $75,000 any member of an unauthorized sect or religious group convicted of a nebulous offense euphemistically referred to as "mental manipulation". Judges will be further empowered to shut down specific groups if two or more members are convicted of these hazy thought crimes.

No reasonable person supports the coercive recruiting tactics employed by cults such as the Unification Church or Moses Berg's Family of God. However, the French law makes little distinction between something as unconscionable as nutritional deprivation or as innocent as repeatedly inviting someone to church.

The Institute on Religion and Public Policy warned in a Crosswalk.com story regarding the French law that proper established methods of evangelism could be outlawed if interpreted as an "exercise in serious and repeated pressure on a person in order to create or exploit a state of dependence."

Fearing the pending wave of oppression ready to sweep across this pivotal European nation, many Protestant groups have dropped the term "evangelical" from their names since that ecclesiastical classification has become something of a dirty word among hypertolerant elites.

Even Pope John Paul II, despite his own ambiguous perspectives regarding Protestantism, has come out in opposition to the French legislation, fearing it will create an atmosphere of unneeded social tension. Other as equally perceptive Catholics, in light of the hostility expressed by militant atheists in that nation since the days of the French Revolution, realize little prevents the law from being used against those adhering to their own interpretation of Christian belief as well. For in the eyes of the radically secular, little separates the fanatic from the sincerely devout regardless of the religion in question.

Though it may not be evident upon an initial view, both the opposition to the McVeigh execution by the militantly secular across Europe and the opposition to basic religious freedoms on the part of French authorities are symptoms of the same theo-philosophical disease.

Having sunk deeper into the quagmire of humanism to a greater extent than even the United States, Judeo-Christian perspectives aren't exactly appreciated for the most part on the European continent. The ironic thing of this is that, in the rush to elevate man above God, intellectuals have inadvertently devalued man by devaluing God. It is this development in man's perceptions about reality that ultimately links the issues of McVeigh's execution and freedom of religion in the mind of the nontheist.

You see, justification for the death penalty finds its foundation in the Biblical idea that, since man is made in the image of God, anyone who sheds innocent blood must be required to atone for such ghastly deeds by forfeiting their own life to duly constituted authorities.

Religious liberty is based upon the idea that, since God exists above and apart from the state, it is not the province of the government to proscribe how the individual relates to providence.

But once God is removed, both of these conceptual frameworks fall apart. In such an instance, it would not really matter what humans did to one another since we have been reduced to the level of savage animals. In the end, McVeigh is no worse than the rescue workers who arrived on the scene to salvage broken bodies and shattered lives and these emergency personnel no better than the fiend taking so many lives.

Likewise, once God has been removed, there is little recourse in appealing to religious liberty because in such de-theized settings the government becomes the ultimate authority able to reconfigure the social contract as it sees fit. One cannot appeal to a higher standard existing apart from the transitory realities of this world if this world is all that exists.

Even more so than the United States, Europe could be said to be a post-Christian society in that it has been more thorough in its effort to expunge the last remaining Judeo-Christian vestiges from its culture. A land that rejoices at the slaughter of innocent babies through abortion yet takes to the street in heated protest against justice being meted to the guilty could just as easily be referred to as "post-commonsense" as well.

Were There Any Good Guys In The Kosovo Conflict?

An honored axiom of international relations posits that the enemy of my enemy is my friend, meaning that it is often expedient to form pragmatic alliances with a regime with whom you have little in common other than a shared adversary. But what happens when the enemy of my enemy also turns out to be my enemy as well?

Jane's, the military and intelligence information publisher, has released findings concluding that the hands of certain Kosovo Albanians are not as clean as they are made out to be in many media reports.

Though many regularly heard of Serbian atrocities during the Balkan hostilities throughout the 90's, little press was given to inappropriate activities on the part of the Kosovo Liberation Army.

According to the *Jane's* findings as reported in *Human Events*, the KLA has orchestrated its own campaign of terror against Kosovoan Serbs as well as against fellow Albanians refusing to assent to the group's policies and tactics.

For example, the Liberation Army assassinated fellow Albanians. And while Americans hear nightly reports of Albanians being forced from their homes at the hands of Serbian aggressors, little is said of Albanian guerillas enacting a similar campaign against innocent Serb civilians.

Much of President Clinton's foreign policy in the Balkans is predicated on the objective of maintaining stability in Europe. However, the introduction of military intervention on the part of the United States may have had the opposite effect.

Already news reports indicate Serb forces have stepped up their campaign of death and destruction in light of the aerial bombardment. And the only thing keeping Russia from entering the conflict on the side of the Serbs against the United States is its own faltering economy and need for Western financial support.

Rogue elements within the Russian military remain a wild card in this scenario as just recently a Russian cargo plane was detained in Azerbaijan for attempting to smuggle fighters out to the highest bidder.

It must be noted that the much-maligned Serbs are not the only destabilizing elements interjected into the situation. Some can, in fact, be found among those the United States is seeking to support.

According to a *700 Club* news broadcast, the Kosovo Liberation Army is a Marxist organization supporting its cause through prostitution and narcotics. Once it has established independence in Kosovo, this group hopes to foment armed revolution among Albanian populations in surrounding countries.

Militant Islamic nations such as Iran hope to ally themselves with these insurgencies to gain a foothold in the very heart of Europe from which to launch subversive activities bent on undermining the "Great Satan" of Western civilization.

Another concern is the impact these kinds of

maneuvers will have on the fundamental purpose of the NATO alliance.

NATO was originally established as a collective security agreement whereby an attack upon one of its signatories would be seen as an attack upon all its members. Neither Serbia nor Kosovo are members of the NATO agreement. By undertaking this effort against the Serbs, this mission in effect turns NATO from a security agreement into some kind of standing European army transcending the scope of its legitimate purpose.

Regarding the Balkans, it has been said this region produces more history than it can possibly consume, meaning it has been marred by considerable warfare and bloodshed. Apart from keeping weapons of mass destruction out of the hands of either side of the conflict, the United States has little national interest there as neither side is pursuing policy objectives beneficial to America's long-term international aspirations.

During the Iran/Iraq War, the United States made the mistake of supporting Saddam Hussein over the Ayatollah Khomeni since at the time Iran was seen as the greater threat. Let's hope the United States is not making the same mistake in another equally volatile part of the world.

Europe A Threat To Democratic Freedoms

It seems the specter of tyranny is never far from once again descending over Europe. Many times it originates in sources one might not normally suspect.

Back in 2000, the conservative weekly *Human*

Events reported the Italian government was considering legislation that would make it a crime to criticize homosexuality on the grounds that such speech might prejudicially influence someone to commit an act of discrimination. Violators could face up to four years in prison.

Proponents of the bill contended it was needed in order to comply with the civil rights standards of the European Union.

It would seem that the European Union does not stand for actual human rights but would rather pursue trendy celebrity causes. Italy is not the only European nation that this transnational body has decided to boss around.

The European Union even took it upon itself to de-legitimize the results of a duly constituted election in Austria when it enacted sanctions because voters there dared to elect the Freedom Party of Joerg Haider to office.

Joerg Haider and the Freedom Party were deemed international pariahs since world opinion concluded that this organization and its leaders allegedly harbored fascist sympathies. The reason: Haider dared to question Austria's liberal immigration policies and dared to postulate that Germans of good character might have served in the Waffen SS. But the icing on the cake was Haider's questioning EU interference in Austrian affairs.

The European Union claimed its diplomatic boycott of Austria had to be enacted for the sake of democracy and pluralism. But is that really the case? Seems this transnational body is the one standing in opposition to a legitimate election; and they cannot argue they did so to prevent extremism.

The Italian Prime Minister that lobbied for the criminialization of the criticism of homosexuality was himself at one time a member of that nation's Communist Party. According to objective history, Communists across the globe have been just as inimical to God-given freedoms and human life as any fascist. So why didn't the European Union try to overturn the outcomes of Italian domestic politics when they veered too far to the Left?

Apparently the European Union is not a champion of tolerance and pluralism but rather of its own social agenda.

The diplomatic ardor of the European Union was not brought to bear against Austria back when that nation enacted a law designed to hinder missionary bodies other than that of the state-sanctioned Lutheran and Catholic churches. Little was said when Germany enacted a similar law designed to counter the spread of Scientology, which also had repercussions for far more acceptable denominations such as the Assemblies of God and the Evangelical Free Church.

Those thinking this kind of hootenanny will confine itself to the more irreligious side of the Atlantic are in for a rude awakening. Already in Canada it is against the law for preachers to speak out against homosexuality in certain instances. And in the United States, federal hate crimes legislation makes intimidating speech part of so-called "hate crimes".

In light of comments by Clinton administration officials directed against an evangelism campaign sponsored by the Southern Baptist Convention reaching out to the Jewish community, it would not be farfetched to predict that one day Christians might be prosecuted for daring to claim that faith in Christ alone is the only way to Heaven on the grounds that such speech constitutes intimidation. Sexual harassment is already determined by a highly subjective and arbitrary standard.

Eschatologists, Bible scholars who forecast the future through the study of Scripture, have often predicted that the current European Union might one day serve as the backbone for the Antichrist's domination of the planet. Only time will tell if such a prediction will prove accurate. However, we do know that those governing the European Union and its allies around the world will present a serious threat to traditional conceptions of liberty throughout the early years of the 21st century.

Troops Might Be Battle-Hardened But leaders Sure Are Thin-Skinned

Throughout American History, cartoonists have used their skill to make poignant statements through the use of symbols that universally tug at the human psyche. However, if some at the highest echelons of government have their way, these artists will no longer be permitted to convey insights informing readers about events of the day but rather forced to use their medium as a way to keep the American people distracted and therefore docile.

To depict what he perceived as the neglected plight of the American fighting man, Tom Toles published a cartoon in the *Washington Post* depicting a soldier having lost his arms and legs in the Iraqi conflict now lying in a hospital bed. Secretary of Defense Donald Rumsfeld is portrayed as the attending physician who turns to the serviceman and says, "I'm listing your condition as battle hardened."

The cartoon was not something pulled entirely out of the cartoonist's imagination. Rather, it was an allusion to the Secretary's reaction to a Pentagon study that the war in Iraq is stretching the armed forces to the breaking point.

But instead of commending Mr. Toles for drawing attention to these comments by the Secretary of Defense that no doubt left a callous ring in the ears of many hearing them, the response to the cartoon (though considerably subdued in comparison to the flap over the Muhammad cartoons in the Muslim world) has degenerated into a case of (at least metaphorically) shooting the bearer of bad news. The criticism of Mr. Toles for daring to express himself extends all the way to the Joint Chiefs of Staff.

In a lettered referenced by *Washington Post* columnist Howard Kurtz, the Joint Chiefs labeled the cartoon as "tasteless". Interestingly, one could make the same case of Rumsfeld's remarks, as those (rather than the Toles cartoon) could be interpreted as making light of the sacrifices made by American troops.

Upon reflecting upon the reaction of the Joint Chiefs of Staff, the critically minded are forced to stop and wonder if these high military officials are concerned about the dignity of those wounded answering the call to defend their country or rather simply want to keep the American people distracted from the truth and thus less critical overall.

People are maimed in war. It is ugly, but it is the truth. Refusing to acknowledge this fact is not going to make it go away and aren't we doing a disservice to those making this sacrifice by shunning what happened to them or hiding them away because the topic makes us uncomfortable?

Some might question if a cartoon is an appropriate venue through which to publicly recognize these heroes. But if the Pentagon has its way, the public won't even be permitted to contemplate the bravery or what some have been called upon to give up for the sake of the nation as even the solemn dignity of a flag-draped coffin is to be shunted away from the view of the American people.

Though this is an important matter dealing with conflicting interpretations of respect and propriety, the response on the part of the Department of Defense is also a cause of concern. Why should the Joint Chiefs of Staff have a public opinion on the matter one way or the other?

Seems that, with the war in Iraq floundering in certain respects and hints made about additional wars with far more formidable adversaries that something should have been done about before we expended our ability to do anything about them, these members of the military elite would not have all that much time to play art critic.

What's The Big Deal?: Peaceniks Overreact To Robertson Comments

Over the course of his broadcast ministry, Pat Robertson has been known to make a number of colorful statements. Among the humorous ranks his insistence that he has prayed hurricanes away from his Virginia Beach compound on a number of occasions.

Most of the time, Robertson's comments go unnoticed by the vast majority of Americans. However, one off-the-cuff remark (actually quite rational upon closer reflection) has generated response beyond reason.

Responding to claims by Venezuela's President Hugo Chavez that the United States was out to get the Latin American malcontent, Pat Robertson jokingly remarked that we might be better off if we obliged him. So enthralled by Third World rabble and emasculated by delusions of multilateralist cooperation, most did not find the one-liner all that amusing.

Yet had Robertson's critics actually taken the time to consider what he had said rather than rush to see how much of a lather they could work themselves up into, they would have discovered his proposal was not all that out of line and actually worthy of additional consideration. In fact, there would have been a time not long ago when Robertson's suggestion would have been applauded as a prudent foreign policy alternative.

Many have expressed outrage that a mere minister and television commentator would call for such a course of action against the leader of another country. However, Hugo Chavez is no genteel statesman to be wined and dined. If anything, he is little more than a petty criminal and not much better than the terrorist scum he is honored to rank among his closest associates.

According to a March 11, 2003 *Weekly Standard* article titled "Comandante Chavez's Friends", Chavez considers Saddam a "brother" and has sought closer diplomatic ties with regimes that sponsor terrorism such as Iran. Even more disturbing, it has been reported that Chavez has given Osama Bin Laden one million dollars and granted sanctuary for an Al Qaeda training facility.

Back at the beginning of the war on terror, President Bush warned that those aiding those engaged in acts of terror would be seen as enemies of the United States and dealt with in a manner befitting such human detritus. Yet the State Department has characterized Robertson's comments as "inappropriate."

Despite the fact that Americans should be more concerned about a government agency thinking its proper role is to condemn remarks by a prominent private citizen (last I checked the Patriot Act had not abolished the First Amendment entirely) than a broadcaster making an offhand policy recommendation, wasn't Robertson merely echoing the President's original sentiments like a dutiful little Republican? Then why are the President's most loyal supporters in the Evangelical conservative community siding with the anti-American beatniks in acting like this single comment has brought the entire moral order crashing down?

The National Council of Churches has labeled

Robertson's comments "appalling beyond belief". Of course they would. That outfit of pastoral pansies never met a Communist they didn't like.

One would hope, however, that the Southern Baptists were made of sterner stuff. Though normally much manlier than the girlie men of the National Council of Churches, even Albert Mohler has gotten onboard the anti-Robertson bandwagon.

Mohler's first argument against Robertson's comments is that they are an embarrassment and don't sound right coming out of the mouth of a Christian leader. Maybe so, but if that is the sole criteria by which we are to judge the propriety of our statements, we'd all close up shop and stay home.

Apart from the need to dance gingerly around the feelings of anti-American foreigners, Mohler points out that "violence can never be blessed as a good." And while he is correct that the Christian should never consider violence lightly, it is interesting that many of the Evangelicals most eager to distance themselves from Robertson's comments are themselves the most enthusiastic supporters of the war in Iraq to oust Saddam Hussein.

Unless God has become a respecter of persons, one would think strategically removing a rogue element disruptive to American interests would be the more Christian thing to do than carry on a war against an entire nation. For while the U.S. military no doubt does its best to minimize casualties, by the law of statistics a number of innocent people are going to die in any war.

Thus, shouldn't Mohler be as critical about his

fellow Christians as gung-ho about calling for the head of Saddam Hussein or any other dictatorial head of state as Robertson is about Hugo Chavez? Just how far is the Christian to go in upholding those in authority?

Would Mohler have spoken out against the plot to kill Hitler even if it could have been prior to the horrors of the Second World War and the Holocaust? More importantly, since manners and propriety have a higher priority in certain hyperpious circles than liberty and even survival, I wonder if Dr. Mohler would care to comment on Winston Churchill teaching his parrot to squawk "F-Hitler."

Some smart aleck will no doubt point out that Hugo Chavez has not killed millions of people nor plunged the world (or at least the Western Hemisphere) into war. Maybe not yet, however, given the Venezuelan radical's questionable associations and stated positions, he does represent a similar destabilizing force and threat to human liberty.

Chavez might not pose much of a threat today, but what about years down the road as the United States continues to weaken through increased Hispanization and hemispheric amalgamation brought about as a result of the "Super-NAFTA conspiracy" surreptitiously being implemented by the Bush administration? And even if Chavez rises to a level no higher than a burr in America's crotch, that would still put him on par with his mentor and confidant Fidel Castro.

Since his doctorate is in historical theology (meaning he knows a bit about the past), would Rev. Mohler care to address the propriety of plans the U.S. had at one time to whack the Cuban tyrant? In the future when historians look back over the reign of Hugo Chavez will they say American Christians did the right thing upholding the Chavez regime and its mass murder, political repression, economic depredation, and prison camps? Already Chavez has issued an enabling act disturbingly similar to that promulgated by Adolf Hitler permitting him to enact any regulation he deems necessary to further his revolutionary objectives.

Contrary to what many Christians seem to believe, there is a world outside the church sanctuary and seldom does it operate by Sunday school rules. Sometimes the things that must be done might not sound that nice splattered across a greeting card or a Precious Moments figurine, but they have to be considered nevertheless if Americans are to continue to enjoy the genteel and respectable lives they have come to expect in a world where such a way of life is the exception rather than the rule.

The Continued Russian Threat

When the Cold War allegedly ended, many Americans thought the world had been transformed into a safe place where the brotherhood of man would come together in chorus singing "We Are The World" while sipping Coca Cola with hands embraced in a circle standing upon a mountaintop. However, the objectivity purchased at the expense of a few years has proven otherwise as concern over nuclear proliferation grows and the former Soviet Union breaks down to such a degree that the constituent parts of the constituent parts seek independence through often violent means as epitomized by the Chechens.

And as this once formidable empire decays into God knows what, certain factions within its borders long for the power and prestige they held during "the good old days". At the same time, the material poverty experienced by the people and the spiritual deprivation caused by the official persecution of religion further exacerbates the situation as the Russian population looks for excuses, even scapegoats, and hope for a future that on the surface appears to grow even darker.

History shows that such poverty coupled with the lack of a firm moral foundation by which to judge the ends and means of leadership is a fertile atmosphere for violent revolutionary movements and demagogues seeking to empower themselves through the broken lives of their followers. The Russia of the late twentieth and early twenty-first centuries is no exception. Some of the various ideologies promising the sky while enslaving the soul include Stalinistic Communism, neo-pagan occultic religions promising salvation through the ancient gods of pre-Christian Russia, anti-Semitism, ultranationalism, and militarism.

Separately, these various movements probably would not gain power and would most likely remain in their individual realms of esoteric abstraction. Some of these movements even contradict one another. However, they do become a threat to world stability and a democracy struggling to be born when a leader can via for their affections and mold the claims of these ideologies into a mass movement winning at least the loyalty of those controlling the resources and positions of power. Such candidates do appear from time to time on the stage of Russian political theater.

At one time, Russian politician Vladimir Zhirinovsky captured the imagination of the Western media and security experts as well as disenfranchised members of the Russian body politic. The background of this man is as fascinating as the threat posed by his ideology. Zhirionovsky was born in 1946 to a White Russian mother and a father who is believed may have been of Jewish origins. Such parentage might not appear all that out of the ordinary, but it does reek of a certain irony as one of the chimes played by Zhirinovsky at various stages of his political career has been the opportunism of anti-Semitism which has often found a receptive ear throughout Russia history. Zhirinovsky was trained at the Afro-Asian Institute of Moscow University where he studied law. Other than these facts, little is known for certain about his early life before his political debut for he has made few friends and surprisingly even fewer enemies who seem to remember him. According to Walter Laqueur in *Black Hundred: The Rise Of The Extreme Right In Russia*, some claim this alleged anti-Semite once worked for a prominent Russian Jewish organization while others (with more accurate speculation perhaps) accuse him of working for the KGB in some capacity.

Zhirinovsky's primary political vehicle and arm on the extreme Russian right is called the Liberal Democratic Party, an ironic euphemism as few would consider it either

"Liberal" or "Democratic". This party (not the only political organization embracing an ultranationalist ideology) does appear to be a faction suited to manipulating a budding democracy in its own favor, a task not that difficult to accomplish as others of similar persuasion often ride around on horseback dressed as Cossacks or wear black shirts while marching in lockstep. William F. Buckley noted in a Jan. 24, 1994 *National Review* column titled, "The Making Of A Miracle" that Zhirinovsky did back Yeltsin's constitution probably because the document is heavy on executive power and Zhirinovsky at that time hoped to one day be that executive.

One theory postulates that the Liberal Democratic Party was established to appeal to individuals fearing the loss of the status they had eked out for themselves under the old Communist system. While this party is not made up of university PhD's or high level government administrators, its message does appeal to those who made society tick such as lower-echelon Communist Party members, police, and factory workers. Walter Laqueur classified many Liberal Democratic Party members as "aggressive elderly men (and) fanatical grandmothers having to make ends meet on...insufficient old age pensions."

One theory postulates that the Liberal Democratic Party was established as a front to maintain the KGB's power base in an age partially given over to certain democratic practices such as multiparty elections. Some experts believe that the Liberal Democratic Party was established to make Communist Mikhail Gorbachev look like a viable alternative compared to the irrational

Zhirinovsky and his grandiose delusions of national martyrdom. However, after the events of August 1991, reforms could not be as carefully orchestrated to preserve the core of the Soviet system and the goal switched from preserving the Gorbachev presidency to opposing the Yeltsin regime and participating in the political process. The hope was to mold the nation through elected office. Laqueur notes former Zhirinovsky allies have brought forth evidence of his KGB connections while others have just as vigorously denied these accusations.

One of the threats presented by Zhirinovsky is the danger he and his crew of malcontents pose to the establishment of democracy and free market institutions. Within the Duma, the Liberal Democratic Party commands a sizeable number of votes and, when combined with the seats controlled by the Communist Party, the two could forge a majority coalition since they concur on more than a few issues warns William F. Buckley. Both parties pine away for days gone by and the restoration of the empire and its glory. Ironically, such a coalition could use the tools of the very democracy they loathe to strangle the reforms designed to abolish the kind of political culture these two parties represent.

Despite the prominence the Liberal Democratic Party enjoyed during the 90's in the Western media as the primary venue of Russian extremism, that particular party represents the ideology's more "moderate" manifestations. For example, some Russian men seeking fellowship and purpose have resurrected the myth of the Cossack. However, there is more at stake here than overgrown boys playing soldier reenacting the Battle of Gettysburg. This development should cause a degree of concern since the Cossacks played a pivotal role in the orchestration of pogroms against the Jews living in Russia; and those attempting to emulate the ideals expressed in this historical lifestyle enunciate an anti-Western position.

Another branch of Russian extremism openly embraces an occultic/neopagan outlook that is not content to remain gazing into crystal balls and reading tarot cards. This branch of the movement wants to resurrect a mythical pre-Christian civilization that they believed marked the zenith of Russian culture. Along with this idea comes the notion that Russian society has been contaminated by Christian and Jewish influences, going so far as to label both the Old and New Testaments as "Jewish fascism". However, as with most other anti-religious kooks, the sanity of the individual must be brought into question as Walter Laqueur notes that the leader of this movement has spent years locked away in mental institutions for murdering and dismembering his wife (115). These individuals, however, cannot be dismissed as mere dabblers in black magic. More than one historian has pointed out the occultic tendencies of the Third Reich to highlight the parallels between these distinct yet similar movements. And to show the seriousness of the situation, a favorite Nazi text, *The Protocols Of The Elders Of Zion*, is popular reading among the ultranationalists.

Another strain of thought making this worldview a threat to European stability is the notion of Pan-Slavism. Many of the extreme Slavophiles, who often buy into other elements of the nationalist ideology, believe that all of the lands inhabited by Slavic peoples should band together regardless of what other ethnic groups and even what other Slavs think, into one state receiving its marching from Moscow. Since the breakup of the Soviet Union, however, non-Russian Slavs such as the Ukrainians have objected to this idea by declaring their own independence according to Natalia Narochnitskaya in an essay entitled "Quelling Nationalism Is Necessary" in *The Breakup Of The Soviet Union* published by Greenhaven Press. Russia has resented losing this area once considered its breadbasket. This intellectual framework of compulsory brotherhood could provide a justification for any aggression Russia might take against its commodity rich neighbor.

A Russia guided by radical nationalists such as Zhirinovsky is a threat to the Western alliance. Those embracing this worldview see attempts at Westernizing the Russian economy as a form of imperialism, and some have gone so far as to demonstrate against the importation of the Snickers bar. However, vocal contempt has not remained confined to peaceful manifestations of cultural disagreement. On numerous occasions, Zhirinovsky has made statements and accusations revealing his loathing of the West that could be construed as threats of war. Mr. Zhironovsky claims that as Russian President he would forcefully take back Alaska from the United States and make Germany a chemical and nuclear wasteland for refusing to grant him an entrance visa according to a William F. Buckley column in the Jan 24, 1994 edition of *National Review*. It does not take Tom Clancy to see the impact such a man or someone like him could have on geopolitical military relations.

Indeed, such personalities and worldviews do have implications for the United States and the Western bloc. After all, words mean things and ideas have consequences whether they reveal considered policy options or an adversary's underlying paradigms. However, the United States can take measures to protect itself and not leave itself wide open for an easy attack. But doing so might mean altering some of our traditional approaches in aiding a nation in such dire straights.

One of the major things the West can do to protect itself from a resurgent Russia or any other belligerent power in the future is to maintain an adequate level of military preparedness. Despite the fact that Communism has supposedly been renounced, that does not mean Russia is no longer a major military power. If anything, that power has become more precarious as Russia's poverty turns offers from rogue nations like Iran to purchase nuclear components and weapons into irresistible temptations. The threat from Russia just doesn't come from these "economic" relationships with third parties. Much of this military threat lies with the Russian army whose members feel a great deal of antagonism towards the West and now their homeland that no longer provides many of its defenders with a respectable living or purposeful occupation. Furthermore, many high ranking officers buy into the nationalists' promises to restore the empire.

When Western nations want to aide countries in these precarious situations, often the policy pursued is one rendering some manner of financial assistance in either the form of grants or loan guarantees. However, such outright transfers of capital could do more to maintain the present system than to change it. While claiming to be against Communism, many of those in positions of leadership rose to prominence under the old system. According to Henry Kissinger in "Western Aide Alone Would Not Strengthen Republics' Economies" in *The Breakup Of The Soviet Union,* aide for the purposes of propping up a dying system could turn out to be an irresistible call to stand by the failed policies of days of yore. Furthermore, financial assistance often goes to line the pockets of those most benefiting from a nation's desperation and depredation, not to create a new socio-political ethos.

In order to ensure the birth of liberty in Russia while crushing the head of the totalitarian serpent, the United States must aide its former and potentially future adversary in laying new cultural foundations. While this can be done in part with assistance from government agencies, the beauty of such a plan is that it could primarily be a private sector endeavor.

Over the course of the twentieth century, Communism robbed the Russian people of many things, the greatest of which was a sense of morality provided by religion as Marxist-Leninist dogma called for blind adherence to the state without religion's moderating influence. The efforts of missionaries who have gone in under liberalized conditions attest to the spiritual hunger of the Russian people as they weep over and kiss the Bibles they have been given. Even some in the Russian government realize the importance of giving the people some firm foundation to stand on since the smashing of old paradigms and the appearance of a listless future.

Education and media officials in their respective agencies, while admitting themselves to be atheists, realize the people need a moral compass, and if a solid one is not offered, anarchy will result. Therefore, as Pat Robertson points out in *Turning The Tide: The Fall Of Liberalism & The Rise Of Common Sense*, American missionaries have been invited to broadcast programs on Russian television and compile educational programs for the schools.

A few commentators and literary figures with religious inclinations have noted the alleged demise of Communism and the ensuing struggle between the Judeo-Christian worldview. If this conflict is not approached seriously, it could result in a new virulent dictatorship ensnaring the souls of the Russian people. Pat Buchanan in a 1993 column titled "Waiting In The Wings" categorized the factions competing for the soul of the Russian people as the following: the neo-pagan nationalists of Zhirionovsky and the Christian patriots following the example of Nobel Prize winning novelist and Soviet dissident Alexander Solzenitsyn.

The extreme nationalist movement in Russia should serve as a reminder to the United States that just because Communism has been severely wounded does not mean the world is at peace and harmony. Some analysts and pundits act like the West can let its defenses down. But we dare not do so in a world characterized by individuals like Zhirinovsky prowling around on the world stage, starved masses craving the purpose provided by a crazed lunatic, and radical Muslims willing to purchase nuclear weapons from such lands so that the starving therein might eat. The United States should assist Russia where it can to take the first steps towards freedom, but policy makers should remember that this baby has a temper and sharp teeth.

Ezekiel 39 speaks of an army from the north coming against God's chosen dwelling in the land of Israel. While many in the modern era dismiss prophecy as superstition, they might not do so as quickly when they learn the anti-Semitic nature of this movement and the fact that Moscow lies directly north of Jerusalem. Could Zhirinovsky or some future protege in fact be the northern prince of this passage known as "Gog, Prince of Magog"? Only time will reveal this ancient mystery.

Hyperpluralism Will Be The Death Of Us

In today's morally confused world, secondary niceties such as tolerance and acceptance are placed on a level above that of fundamental necessities such as the preservation of the nation and even survival itself.

The announcement that the contract to administer a number of America's most strategic ports had been rewarded to a company from the United Arab Emirates galvanized Americans across the political spectrum. Michael Savage was discussing the issue with Charles Schummer as if the two were old friends and the host even joked about inviting Hillary Clinton onto his program if it would help spread the word about the unsettling development.

Yet despite this threat to all Americans, ABC decided to frame the issue as one of possible xenophobia. Here, with one of the gravest threats to ever face the internal security of the United States as officials at the highest levels essentially handed our most strategic points of entry on a silver platter to the operatives of a nation sympathetic towards the terrorist enemy, the news bureau of one the largest networks grew all a twitter whether or not the people of the United States are sufficiently broadminded and globalist in their outlook.

As is becoming more characteristic of the Bush administration, concerned Americans have once again been reminded that theirs is not to reason why but theirs is but to do or die in that as loyal citizens we are to trust Glorious Leader without question; and it probably won't be long until we are told (as in the case of the wiretapping program) that to even mention the ports agreement is to give aide and comfort to the enemy and endanger homeland security. Already administration mouthpieces are claiming that, while the trade arrangement posed no threat to the American people, we are to be granted precious little insight into how the decision was arrived at that even the Secretary of Defense or the President did not know much about. Makes you wonder who is really running the show if even the foremost officials of the executive branch were among the last to know.

With an enemy adept at exploiting any weakness in our defenses with a fanaticism that would put many a Soviet agent to shame, the American people have the right to know why their own government is so naive as to think that in the course of a twenty day investigation that this potential front company is to be trusted with access straight into the hearts of some of America's most concentrated centers of population.

Even if those running the Dubai Ports Company

were as peaceable as Lancaster County Pennsylvania Dutch, why shouldn't we suspect that their swarthy kinsman and coreligionists won't endeavor to infiltrate the port company? Administration propagandists assure us everything would be OK as the Coast Guard would be there to protect us.

But if Al Qaeda operatives infiltrated the company over time, wouldn't these minions of perdition be able to crack the Coast Guard's defenses eventually? All it takes it takes is just one nuclear or radiological bomb to get through.

To the President, it might just be one big oops because, apart from a little momentary regret, it will eventually all be put behind him as he will be whisked to some ultrasecret underground or beneath the sea bunker. Those residing near the ports wouldn't be so fortunate, for if they're lucky they'd be dead as that might be preferable to a life of radiation-induced sickness, the loss of all of ones possessions, and life in a FEMA relocation camp that would make the New Orleans Superdome in the aftermath of Hurricane Katrina look like a stay at Cinderella's Castle in Disney World.

It will be average Americans opposed to the Dubai proposal and decisions like it that would have to live with the consequences. If anything, should a nuclear holocaust befall the United States, elites favoring such plans would rise like the Morlocks in *The Time Machine* by H.G. Wells over a decimated world only to tighten their grip over the impoverished masses that remain.

Isn't this the same government already charged with securing the nation's borders? Just look at the fine job being done there and you'll see just how safe our ports would have been had they been handed over on a silver platter to a bunch of foreigners.

Expanding on the insinuations of xenophobia as embodied by the ABCNews.com headline, Islamic front groups have picked up on the suggestion and turned to beating the drums of racism, knowing like all good subversives that this is the magic password to bring the American political process to a screeching halt.

One Arab columnist wrote of the widespread response to the port fiasco, "Islamophobia is rising and has become like an infectious disease that spreads...in the West." And another Arabist said of those opposed to the deal, "they are reopening 9/11 wounds turning this into an Arab-Muslim conspiracy to control the lives of Americans."

Flying jetliners into national landmarks and deliberately killing thousands of innocent noncombatants kind of has a tendency to create a sense of distrust and suspicion, especially when millions upon millions of those of the same religious persuasion as the perpetrators celebrate the atrocity as some kind of sacred undertaking. And even if no overt acts of terrorism resulted from the transfer of the ports to a foreign power other than those among the civilized brotherhood of Western nations, surrender of these centers of power and commerce still represent a dangerous infiltration of American society.

A significant portion of history teaches that that the most dangerous conquerors are not necessarily those that come in with their guns blazing but rather those that come in a much more subtle manner. Thus from a certain perspective, Americans should be more concerned about those Muslims with a more long-term outlook that could employ a seemingly peaceful strategy until they reach a critical number and stab America in the back as these more quiet revolutionaries could do something far worse than just about anything their more homicidal kinsman could dream up, namely the destruction of America's Judeo-Christian culture and the elimination of the system of constitutional liberties that arose from it.

Those that say Islam is not out to conquer the West in general and the United States in particular either don't know what they are talking about or are either part of the organized conspiracy. For while Islamic front groups attempt to put up a respectable democratic face, it does not take much effort to discover what's really beneath the surface.

Groups such as the Council on Islamic American Relations and their ilk claim they merely want to participate in the nation's democratic process. However, such a plea is about as trustworthy as when it fell from the lips of Bolshevists from whom many of these contemporary insurgents learned duplicitous forms of conquest.

In the August 4, 2003 edition of WorldNetDaily.com, Christian Arab Anis Shorrash, a member of the Oxford Society of Scholars, detailed what he believes to be the Islamic plan for American by the year 2020. Key points of this program include the termination of America's freedom of speech through the passage of hate crimes legislation and, as John Hagee pointed out in a series of sermons on Islam, the eventual replacement of the U.S. Constitution with a document based on Sharia law. Islamists hope to accomplish this through a number of steps, particularly via a massive demographic shift brought about through unbridled immigration and the seduction of gullible American women for breeding purposes.

Already Muslims have taken over vast swaths of Detroit, Michigan and Camden, New Jersey. They have also begun to take over entire industries to bring about these kinds of changes from the bottom up.

Often Americans are fed a steady barrage of propaganda that a continuous flow of foreigners must be allowed into the United States to fill vacant jobs lazy Americans are no longer willing to perform. Is it really that Americans are no longer willing to or no longer permitted?

During the 1990's in my hometown, the executives of a major chain of gas stations came through and laid-off all of the Americans employed at the particular station. Every last replacement was of Middle Eastern origin.

Though Scripture teaches that all human beings are equal in that that they are created in the image of God and share a common ancestry, the way in which groups of people come to live in culture and civilizations are not. It might not be politically correct to say it, but if America's ethnic makeup is tampered with too much skewering things in favor of nationalities not exactly known for a track record of constitutional republican government, the freedoms we now enjoy as Americans might very well cease to exist.

Such words don't sound very pleasing to

contemporary ears conditioned to hear of absolutist tolerance and hyperdiversity as the highest social values, trumping even survival it now seems. However, conditions in Europe are a foreshadow of things to come if the United States does not come to its senses about whom we allow to enter into our midst.

In the same way that Muslim men woo American women into thinking their suitors are adorable and charming only to become abusive despots in the home once married, those of the faith under consideration here have shown up on the doorstep of the West promising to become good little pluralists only to attempt to takeover the whole show once their numbers reach a certain level.

Part of the deal of living in a free society where one has the right to say what one wants and to believe as one chooses is having to put up with hearing things we don't necessarily want to about the things we hold most dear. Once Muslims reach a certain number in a given Western country, they have certainly gotten the saying what they want part down; however, to say they need a little work on putting up with the things they don't want to hear is an understatement. For the extent to which Islamic malcontents have refused to accept this responsibility, they are endangering the lives and liberties of each and everyone of us.

Islamists have gone beyond their rights in a number of European nations to speak out against policies and conditions they find inimical to their way of life. This has become so serious that they have begun to infringe upon the rights of those with whom they disagree.

Theo Van Gogh was shot for producing a

documentary critical of Islam. Mobs laid waste to much of France over two youths shot by police. Similar riots have broken out over a number of cartoons depicting Muhammad. Muslims in Indonesia went on a murderous rampage simply because Jerry Falwell dared to call Muhammad a terrorist.

Though rampaging ragheads might be what ultimately brings about the nation's physical demise, the process of decline began long before. Islamic fanaticism and Hispanic radicalism stand on the verge of conquering more sophisticated industrialized nations simply because they want them more than the current inhabitants. For while these competing cultures are willing to do whatever it takes to seize the lucrative prize of world domination, those that ought to be the most vigorous at least vocally in rallying to the cause of Christendom (namely male Fundamentalists) fritter on about manners such as what soupspoon to use like a bunch of old grannies in a retirement home.

In early 2006, I wrote a column titled "British Flap Their Pie Holes Over Hot Cross Buns" about efforts in merry ole England on the part of the hypertolerant to remove hot cross buns from public school menus for fear of, its was stated, offending Jehovah's Witnesses and no doubt Muslims as well who (unlike the peaceful Witnesses) have no qualms about setting cars on fire and lopping off heads on videotape when their feelings get hurt. Thinking those self-identified as "Fundamentalists" would enjoy the commentary, I mistakenly decided to post the essay in on one of the movement's most prominent Internet forums.

Instead of welcoming me within their midst as an ally or kindred spirit and praising my wit, I was roundly castigated on how it was my Christian obligation to bow to the preferences of my spiritual betters. Fundamentalists, at one time, had a reputation for not backing down from a fight. However, now it seems many of the movement's leaders are no more manly than those in their counterpart denominations where the ministers wear frilly robes and lacey collars when standing in the pulpit.

One responded with all the courage of some blubbering peacenik cowering in the corner blathering about how nuclear annihilation will rain down on America if we don't unilaterally disarm and how September 11th was somehow our fault blurted, "...if you want to make it difficult for Americans ministering in the UK, keep posting things like this on U.S. sites."

I doubt my meager columns will be the reason why the West was lost. As such, I do not have a responsibility to have my writings vetted by some missions board.

Often in Fundamentalist and Evangelical circles, it is assumed that the only legitimate form of ministry is that conducted within institutional church settings and even in Protestant circles common believers are expected to, shall we say, kiss the ring of the pope. Usually this translates in bowing to the preferences of missionaries and pastors even when such demands are not clearly spelled out in the pages of Scripture.

As such, my "derogatory language" (I guess "pie hole" is not a phrase used all that much around the baptismal font) and failure to role over on command just because someone on a church payroll told me to, I was told I would be barred from the forum if my attitude persisted because my comments were "inconsistent with Scripture" and "unnecessarily insulting". Ironically, such admonishments were rendered by a pastor whose church belonged to the American Council of Christian Churches, an ecclesiastical fellowship founded by Carl McIntire as an alternative to the National Council of Churches.

While Carl McIntire should be remembered for standing up for the Christian faith in the 20th century against Marxist and modernist infiltration of the church and society, it is highly doubtful every last word out of his mouth was characterized by the same degree of obsequiousness and unabrasiveness demanded of me by the "Pansymentalists". For by the end of his 95 years upon the earth, McIntire not only masterfully excoriated his opponents but, since most gifts and talents have a downside, he must have had a hard time turning it off as well because by the time of his passing, he had parted ways with almost everyone he had considered a friend or an associate. While it is not my place to decide on the propriety of such personal decisions, I am not the one going around threatening that everyone has to be all smiles and sunshine or face ecclesiastical ostracism.

The forum moderator concluded, "Your fellow member deserves more respect than you have shown him. He is working to give the Gospel to the culture you are broadly deriding." And why exactly don't I deserve the same kind of respect, as frankly I was not the one to start the fight?

While I don't exactly fritter about from church to church with an outstretched tin cup telling everyone how holy I am or send fundraising letters to former friends whose existence I have not acknowledged in years informing them just how much they are blessed by the Lord for having this opportunity to send me money to fiance some foreign escapade as many a missionary does, aren't I also working to give society the Gospel message? While those fake plastered-on smiles might work for some, it turns off just as many others. As such, under the Biblical admonition to be all things to all men, don't we have an obligation to make room for those preferring a plain-spoken or realistic approach to the world or as John Warwick Montgomery termed it "Christianity for the tough minded"?

America's enemies are not the kind of people to say "please" and "thank you" or help little old ladies across the street. As such, Americans must arouse themselves mentally for the challenge that lies ahead. And if the price of such a state of awareness is an occasional phrase that some might find a little shocking, then so be it. Unsettled sensibilities are better than an environment where no one is allowed to say anything at all as a result of surrendering this great nation to those that hate both God and man.

www.ingramcontent.com/pod-product-compliance
Lightning Source LLC
Chambersburg PA
CBHW020303290526
45784CB00003B/1340